The Grist Anthology of New Writing

edited by Michael Stewart
associate editor David Gill

Grist Books 2009

Editor	Michael Stewart
Associate Editor	David Gill
Cover Design	Tom Rawcliffe
Inner page design	Ruth Inglis
Judges of the Grist Short Story Competition	Joanne Harris
	Mark Ellis
	Michael Stewart
Judges of the Grist Poetry Competition	Simon Armitage
	David Gill
	Gaia Holmes

The Grist Anthology of New Writing is published by Grist Books, in association with The University of Huddersfield.

Please note that all the work published here is previously unpublished with the exception of The Door by Helen Simpson (published in *Constitutional*) and Swans by Jim Greenhalf (published in *The London Magazine*).

www.hud.ac.uk/grist

Copyright © the authors 2009

All rights reserved

Many thanks to the University of Huddersfield for their continuing support

ISBN: 978-0-9563099-0-7

About Grist

Grist provides a unique platform for emerging writers. By publishing emerging writers alongside some of the best known names in literature, Grist offers a unique opportunity for those starting out in their writing careers.

The winners of the Grist short story competition 2009

1st – **Indigo Runway**
Jess Richards

2nd – **Martin In A Hole**
Brindley Hallam Dennis

3rd – **Stinky**
Ben Cheetham

The winners of the Grist poetry competition 2009

1st – **The Birdbath's Saying Dive**
Jonathan Asser

2nd – **Fishing Trip**
Hilary J Murray

3rd – **Poem For The Love Lane Crow**
Gareth Durasow

Foreword

As a writer and teacher of writing I am constantly on the lookout for materials, materials to inspire me and materials to inspire others. *Grist* began very simply with a desire to bring together a collection of the best new writing in the creative field, but in the process to place emerging writers with established writers and in so doing, to give emerging writers a helping hand, to shine a light on their work and to give them recognition. My thanks then go to both the writers who submitted work through the competition and to the generosity of the established writers here who donated their work: Simon Armitage, Helen Simpson, Lemn Sissay, Ian McMillan and John Boyne.

When I put the call out for submissions in the summer of 2008 the work trickled in and by October I was worrying that there wouldn't be enough material. The deadline was looming: the end of November. Then the work started to arrive in droves. By the deadline there were thousands of stories and poems.

I did some of the initial sifting, discounting all those stories that began, 'it was morning when she woke up. She got out of bed, got dressed and went down for breakfast.' Or, 'dear little Philippa was in the park picking peonies in her pink bonnet when she came across the prettiest squirrel.' These, I have to say, were gently and affectionately tossed in the bin. Also to be quickly discarded were those pen portraits to a member of the family, 'my uncle Bob was the nicest bloke you could ever meet. He used to come for his tea every Thursday.'

In addition, anything written in crayon or blood, or anything that used a fancy typeface, was often an early indicator of poor quality. Anything that began with three paragraphs of description of the weather or came in a folder tied with a bow... don't ask me why those stories that came in a folder tied with a bow were so awful, or why fancy typefaces often hide something outright barbarous, some things you just can't account for.

Thankfully I was helped on the way by the judges who I'd like to thank here. So a big thank you to Simon Armitage, Joanne Harris, David Gill, Gaia Holmes and Mark Ellis. I really am very grateful for all your hard work, generosity and expertise. Without you this collection simply would not have happened.

William Blake said that, 'he who does not imagine in minute particulars does not imagine at all.' It's something I tell my students all the time. Show don't tell is the old maxim. The stories and poems in this collection represent some of the most daring, distinctive and boldly imaginative writing in English today. In every case I was impressed by how they dramatised events, in short, how they imagined in minute particulars, and I am very pleased and proud to be able to offer you this collection.

New writing is always a challenge for publishers, but an anthology of short fiction and poetry seems a particular challenge. We are very fortunate at *Grist* – we do not have any commercial pressures. We can do things differently, and on that note my final thanks go to The University of Huddersfield for their ongoing support. I hope you the reader will find this book an adventure. I hope you will be surprised and delighted by its audacity, but most importantly I hope you enjoy all it has to offer.

Michael Stewart
Editor

Contents page

The Birdbath's Saying Dive Jonathan Asser	11
Indigo Runaway Jess Richards	13
Fishing Trip Hilary J Murray	17
Martin In A Hole Brindley Hallam Dennis	18
Poem For The Love Lane Crow Gareth Durasow	28
Stinky Ben Cheetham	30
The Flight Of Swallows Kate Dempsey	39
Song Thrush Jacquie Shanahan	41
The Door Helen Simpson	42
Thin Red Line Lynn Roberts	50
The View From Darwin Gardens Jim Greenhalf	51
A Dangerous Crossing Penny Aldred	52
Brothers Of The Hood Len Evans	59
Dreaming Of Carpet Cleaner Ruth Inglis	60
Today I Changed A Baby Glenn Carmichael	61
Deadheading Nina Boyd	64
The End Of The Pier John Boyne	65

The Shave Glynis Charlton	80
Da's Dublin 2008 Beda Higgins	82
26,298 Mick Haining	83
I Love Martin Wickham	87
Love Poem 32 Justine Warden	88
Sonnett 155 Anna-Marie Vickerstaff	89
Between Floors Cath Humphris	90
Story Without Meaning John Brown	96
Teaching Beginners Poetry Fiona Durance	103
This Is Disaster Poetry Andrea Tang	104
Smoke Me A Tune Holly Oreschnick	105
Yawna's Tale Mark Ellis	106
The Elephant Who Came To Tea Ami Roseingrave	114
Swans Jim Greenhalf	116
Dipps, The Goose And The Gooley Goo Timothy Allsop	117
Conjuror Karl O'Neil	124
Paper Flowers Julie Mellor	126
Unicorns Don't Have Wings Kyrill Potapov	127
Buying Into The Property Market Skye Loneragan	135

House Clearance Gaia Holmes	136
Blessed Gaia Holmes	137
Vanilla Grave Dirt Christopher Parvin	138
Travel Writing Ian McMillan	147
A Room To Write In Gillian Davis	148
The Citizens Louis Malloy	150
Show And Tell Simon Armitage	160
Snappy Paul Duncan	163
Dad Andrew McMillan	171
Don't Step On The Cracks John Glander	173
Lost And Found Kelly Stanger	180
I Think My Muse Is Having An Affair Kelly Stanger	181
Tits Like Elephants' Ears Natalya Lowndes	182
Rough Gaia Holmes	188
Smooth Gaia Holmes	189
The Unknown Boxer Shorts Katherine Spink	190
Rest Lemn Sissay	198
As Charles Bukowski Might Have Said Jim Greenhalf	199
Biographical Notes	200

The Birdbath's Saying *Dive*

Jonathan Asser

Saturday evening, I'm on my roof.
Brick exhales the day's quota of sunshine.
My Camel cigarette out glows a moon
that's harvest orange, edging a high-rise.

Textured bitumen dimples my butt.
Ants patrol a Russian vine's tips.
Ambulances wang in counterpoint
to traffic-light bleepers. Bach drifts up.

Dave, armed-robber turned facilitator,
who does SVI work with me part-time
for Camden probation, said I must learn
to understand the Little Jo inside.

A person opposite strips off, does tai chi.
Garlic wafts from someone's veg stir-fry.
Moths buffet sensor lights bursting
on to prickles of in-house cacti.

Dave stole a nanny goat when he was ten
and coaxed it on a train for Marylebone.
Policemen put the goat in a riot van.
Dave torched a batch of self-build mobile homes.

I stand and traverse coping towards air.
Skylights each side slope away in gloom.
I reach the end, flex crêpe-soled suede footwear
over the edge, experience a spasm.

Snails I can't make out three floors below
attack their thirst in two inches of birdbath.
Testicular frissons play the banjo.
I grip another Camel in my teeth.

Indigo Runaway

Jess Richards

I run away the day they're going to push up the sky. Everyone's outside making plans. They don't usually want any mention of the sky because it's so low in some places they have to hunch over to walk. All my life it's been this unspeakable thing, this trouble all the adults have. The children and teenagers, like me, we've learned to collect whispers about it. We've become spies, trading buttons, mirrors, toys, whatever we can find, for secrets.

For weeks the adults haven't talked about anything else, it's like the floodgates have opened. All these words they've kept hidden from us for years are spilling out through the whole community. We're caught in a torrent of words. How terrible it's been for them to live like this. How their world will be transformed once they can walk tall without fear of banging their heads, and the horrific after effects. I've nearly stopped growing, but I'm still short and haven't hit my head on it yet. They say it feels as if there are a thousand needles which pierce the scalp, the feeling of crashing into it. This lasts for days, and then the blue-white cloud shaped bruises appear across the face. We call them sky tattoos. They take weeks to fade away, longer if they're really deep ones.

My grandfather hit his head on the sky three times in one day and the sky tattoos spread across his head and all over his body. He slept for a month without being able to speak at all, and when he woke up, he could only say words that were all to do with the weather. He rambled endlessly about rain and sunbeams, storms, fog and rainbows, cloud formations. It took months of us listening to him closely to figure out if he'd got any proper thoughts any more, or if he'd just gone simple. They didn't notice I was there, the adults. I sat on the floor in the corner of his room, spying from behind his rocking chair.

I wanted to understand what the sky had done to him. His language had changed completely. Rain descriptions, like squally, showers and torrential meant things he didn't want, and the word 'no'. When he was enjoying something, usually thick soup or steamed pudding, he would laugh during spoonfuls and shout joyfully about sunshine, splattering food all over his duvet.

Rainbows were used when he was pleased to see someone. He'd get lost in describing the colours in different ways, depending on who he was talking to. Red, he described as boiling point, scalding bathtubs, desire and lust. Green led to descriptions of the temperature required for the germination of seeds, hope and possibility. Blue was ink, loss, persuasion. When he once saw me curled in the corner watching him, he started rambling about indigo runaways. I didn't have a clue what he meant. When he was annoyed or confused he would mutter for hours about cloud formations. Cumulonimbus, altostratus, cirrus... when he started talking storms, it meant that he'd lost the plot and we all ran for shelter. He'd hurl anything within arm's reach. These were the only days he'd leave the house. One day he tore out five fir trees with his bare blue-white hands. I think that's where they got the idea about pushing up the sky from, though everyone is claiming the original plan as their own. He is left with permanent faded sky tattoos all over him, like a wooden table covered in blurred stains from spilled ink.

The sound of axes being sharpened slice the air like the wail of peacocks. I'm packing my bag alone in my room. I hunt out useful things: blanket, knife, clothes, food. Outside my low window the fir trees are about to be cut down. I can see them in the distance. It's as if they somehow know. The trees have prepared themselves. Some of them have sucked in their roots, as if they're holding their breath. I always imagined their roots being as huge underground as the tree is above it, creating tunnels shaped like lungs under the earth. These trees stretch further than the sky, pierce right through it and disappear into whatever is above. They make holes in the sky and the sky closes round their trunks, shutting the top of the tree away from us.

I once tried to climb a tree, and when I got to the place where the sky began I was too scared to touch the sky. It makes the strangest sounds. I sat in the tree for hours, smelling fresh growth in the branches. I watched the iridescence in the sky subtly change. My face was just an inch below its surface. No one came looking for me. Here, no one glances upwards. The sky sounds like an instrument, like the wind, like bells. It collects all the sounds we make and keeps them inside it, changing them into weather conditions. Clouds, storms, snow, rain and sunshine. Underneath all these sounds, and the echoes of all the words we have ever said, there is a soft base, a beating pulse. The sky keeps all the tree sounds as well, creaks and snaps, the papery flutters of leaves. And a low slow drone which can only be the sound the tree makes when it's growing.

When I was little I burrowed holes into the roots of these trees, hiding places for the possessions I wanted to keep secret. My mum used to routinely find all my hiding places at home.
I never knew what she expected to discover, but whatever it was, she wasn't going to. I ran my fingers over the cracked trunks yesterday when I dug them out again. The book I read to my younger brother, Bill, about a chicken and the sky falling in. Now half rotten, damp, with the rich scent of soil. A rusted tin box full of pictures Bill drew of me, my mouth red and singing. Scrawled crayon lines of me and him crawling like cats, sitting on the floor under the low sky. He drew the sky into all of his scribbles, till the adults took his crayons away. A small bent metal hoop, from where we rolled it along the ground so hard it ricocheted off a stone and hit the sky, falling down shimmering and twisted. My collection of buttons in a blue glass jar.

These go in my bag as well. I don't want to see them cut down the trees. I don't want to hear them being pulled down out of the sky or sliced from the ground. My room is empty now, just a mattress, a cracked empty vase and a photo of my mum that she always insisted was kept on my mantelpiece. Her eyes have always followed me round this room, as they are this morning. I breathe in.

It's time to go. I put the picture in my bag. Mum never speaks. She uses her hands to talk to me. I don't know what happened to her. I just know she's not spoken a word since I've been alive, and walks stooped lower than anyone else. She has just one permanent sky tattoo. In the picture she is hunched over, with the sky tattoo on her lips. That mark has been there for years. Did she kiss the sky once? I will never know now, she has gone with all the others to cut out the trees which they'll use to push up the sky. I don't know what'll happen. It could fall down completely and kill us all instantly. We could get stuck in it. Lost in the permanent pain of those needles, coloured entirely blue with sky tattoos. Surrounded by iridescent colours and the intense sounds that came from us in the first place. We could hear all the words we'd ever said repeated back to us over and over again. We could become the weather. It could take away our language and give us a new one, like my grandfather. Or it could work, their plan. The sky pushed up so high I will never again climb a tree and be able to hear what it sounds like. But I'm not going to see it happen. If I'm not killed because the sky falls down, or lost in it forever, I won't be coming back here, even though I've not said goodbye. I'm going to just keep running.

Fishing Trip

Hilary J Murray

In my cave I'm subtle metal,
tangerine wire stretched to a bald grin.
You should have stayed a land-lubber;
your lobster-pots-baskets to store –
late apples. Though russet peel may
squeak, scale off from mushy pulp
and you can't eat rot, rust or wicker.

Come to my fish lips – gollop. Once
mere roe, a blob in spawn, I grew
through each blip of a tadpole cycle.
Shook dewdrop mucus from match-head
limbs; struck out, legged it up chalk cliffs
to high and dry flint. And lay there:
mother-of-pearl opening, yes –

immaculate. Yet wrenched apart.
Thighs nut-cracker wide, shut, wide;
highs like nothing I'd known before.
But tedium encroached, blank
surface of the drop-dead gorgeous.
I couldn't help it; air-breathing
stems ceased to attract. So un-

double me, give me my stigma back:
the hustle of the ugly, my rustling
fish-tail quiver. Quick. Slash
your net. Or I'll lunge, thrash,
lash you as I jaw right through it
and quit this tidal cave for good –
to fin through the soft body of the sea.

Martin In A Hole

Brindley Hallam Dennis

Martin had taken to living in a hole in the ground. Not a comfortable hole. It was a nasty dirty wet hole, filled with ends of worms, and an oozy smell.

It was a hole of his own making. He had dug it out of the clay bank that tilted down from the house, spade-full by spade-full, among the roots of old apple trees through which he had sliced spitefully with the spade's sharp edge. He had told them that he was making an orangery. He had seen an orangery at some castle or other belonging to the National Trust that they had visited one summer many years ago.

That had been a cool and gloomy space, shielded from the prying eyes of the world by thick columns of marble, heavily veined and entwined with climbing plants that wound their way out of large terracotta pots, and had dark, glossy leaves, and were of a variety unknown to him, but which he assumed to be a species of vine. The floor had been made of grey stone slabs over which lichen and moss were spreading in circles and semicircles, emanating from the dark crevices between them, as if there were a sea of molten greenery beneath that was being forced slowly but surely from the nether world into the upper by the pressure of some rising tide. There had been no oranges, so far as he could ascertain.

How long can you wait? How long can you maintain, despite silences, despite not seeing their faces, despite not being, ever, in their company, the love of any person? Years? Those parted by wars, by repression, by miscarriages of justice, by mistaken turnings taken in darkened rooms under the influence of alcohol, or lust, or fear, will tell you.

He had liked that orangery. He had felt comfortable in its damp, unproductive space. Hidden by its shadows he had watched the other visitors drifting along the border paths in the hot sunshine outside. Though none had turned to look directly at him it had been as if his shadowy presence had somehow deterred them from approaching his cave, as if it were the lair of some mythical beast.

The hole that he had dug into the orchard bank was not as big. He would have needed a mechanical digger for a week to make such a big hole as that. He would have needed to take out several of the trees. He would have needed to insert props of some sort to hold up the roof of the excavation. He would have needed boards, or planks at the very least, to reinforce the clay walls lest they might give way and engulf him.

Robert found Jane at the kitchen table. Her eyes were rimmed with red as if she had been out in a cold wind, or had rubbed chilli powder into them by mistake while preparing a continental dish with a spicy sauce. The kitchen blinds had been drawn down, not because the day was bright, but because having them that way deterred her from standing at the kitchen sink constantly and looking out over the garden to where the bank tipped away down into the orchard.

'Where is he?'

'Out there.'

'How are you?'

'I don't know.'

'How's Merle?'

'Quiet. She doesn't understand. She knows something's wrong.'

'How long has it been now?'

'Two weeks, ten days. I'm losing track.'

He had worked at it in the evenings, accompanying each spade thrust with the grunt of a weight lifter. Huh! So that the thump of the spade into the earth had an echo, as if the sound had rebounded from his body. Huh! He did not work fast, but he kept at it as the light faded. The evenings were drawing out, as summer approached. So his sessions grew longer, a few minutes a day, a few more than the actual lengthening of the period of the light, for he worked each evening a little further into the time of darkness. He rigged up a lamp, running a cable down from the house, looping it through the filling blossom of the apple trees as if he were stringing fairy lights in preparation for a party. This enabled him to work longer, digging to one side of his own shadow, the spade blade shining briefly as it passed through the beam into the blackness of the hole it was making. The hole remained pitifully small, for all his efforts, and a pile of spoil grew untidily in front of it. The tree roots took several blows to sever. Huh! Huh! Huh!

'I'll go and talk to him.' Robert said.

He had been digging for a fortnight before he stayed out for the night. By that time he had been working until well into the night and Jane had not missed him until she woke in the morning. Perhaps if she had questioned him at that time it would have been nipped in the bud, but she had not, and he had stayed out the next night too. After that the moment had passed.

You cannot tell people that your husband is sleeping in a hole in the garden, not unless they are very close to you, not unless they are complete strangers. Most of our lives are not spent in the company of those who are very close to us. Most of our encounters with strangers do not offer up the opportunity for disclosing such information. That at least was the case with Jane's life. She saw Martin. She saw Merle. Husband. Daughter. She saw Jim, the postman. She saw the girl with the big earrings and the small scar at the local mini-market checkout. She saw the ladies of the village hall coffee morning. Neighbours. She saw the solicitors and other secretaries at the law firm in town where she worked, part time, three days a week. Work colleagues. She saw Sandra. Sandra almost qualified for the telling.

She saw Robert, occasionally. Old friend of the family. He had been Martin's friend in the beginning. That had been twenty years ago. He had not been her friend. She had not been his. That had developed through the stages of resentment, tolerance, grudging acceptance, warmth, and, since about five years before, when she had been ill, that form of intimacy which does not require, at least within any given time parameter, the mutual exposure of disrobing and orgasm.

'He's taken to sleeping in the garden.'

Pause.

'Not, under the stars. Nothing like that.'
Pause.
'He's dug a hole.'
'A hole?'
Pause.
'I don't know what to do.'
'I'll come round.'

The hole was big enough to reverse a small car into. The spoil had been tipped to both sides of what must be taken for the entrance, and had been smoothed, graded might be the technical word, to curve, like the arms of a croissant, into the surrounding slope. At its deepest point the clay floor was perhaps six foot below the lip of turf that overhung it. A lattice of tree roots offered some support. It was not a roof, merely an overhang, six inches wide, a foot at most. A band of darker, moister earth ran around the rim, a spade's blade depth of it. Below that it was clay, orange, red, depending on the light. It glistened slightly, but water does not move easily through clay. The walls could not, by any stretch of imagination, have been described as running wet. That is the danger of clay. It holds the water. Holds back the weight of water in the hillside behind it. That is why clay heaves, gives way, when the volume of water swells, grows, as temperatures change.

'That doesn't look safe to me.'
Safe.

The appearance of safety is something that we all fail, if statisticians are to be believed, to match up with its actuality, but it is the appearance that matters to us, when all is said and done. It is what we are comfortable with.

'Is it finished?'
'Nearly. It's only temporary.'
'Then what?'
'I haven't thought that through yet.'
'Until then?'
'That's what it's for.'
'I see.'
'It's all a matter of how far you're prepared to go.'

It is important to keep your spade clean. A stainless steel

spade is the best, but even they, if not kept clean, will become clogged and heavy with the sticky mass of clay. Clay may be almost any colour, from white through to black. There are blue clays, clays that are almost green. Mostly it is found in the red-orange band of the spectrum. The colour reflects the chemical make-up of the material, but the term itself refers to the size of the particles. Clay particles are tiny. A spoon full of clay particles, it is said, would have the same surface area, if unfolded and spread out, as a football pitch. I forget which size spoon. I forget which version of football. It is because the particles are so small that water has such difficulty in moving through it. That is why it is so heavy, so crushing, so suffocating.

By now you must be wondering why I am telling you all this. What difference does it make to me? What difference might it make to you? I'm not sure I have answers to those questions. It was the hole itself, the need for it, what it seemed to be, that made me think the story was worth telling.

'Are you planning to stay out here, until then?'
'Not planning, exactly.'
'But you probably will.'
'Probably.'
'Jane's worried about you.'
'Yes.'
'Have you finished digging?'
'I think so.'
'That's good.'
Pause.
'Is it cold?'
'Compared to what?'
'The house?'
'No.'
'Come on.'

There are no worms deep down inside the clay. Worms do not live on clay. They ingest it, eat it if you like, to use as a grinding paste to break down their real food, green stuff, dying organic material. They also eat the remains of insects, small animals, meat. They go deep to avoid cold weather, go shallow to avoid drowning. They travel across the boundary between the clay and the darker soil above, but they do not live in the clay. Those that wriggle out of the topsoil at the face of the hole fall down into it. If they are not eaten there, or drowned in the small pools of water that lie in the angle between the wall faces and the floor, they move to one side or the other, seeking out the organically enriched layer. There are always some worms in the hole, dead, or moving. Martin was not bothered by them.

'You must get wet, when it rains.'

'Yes. Pain, that.'

'You can't carry on like this, you know.'

'I know. That's the trouble. It's like everything else, temporary.'

'Why don't you come back up to the house? Have a cup of tea.'

'Time. No time.'

'No time for tea?'

'No time to explain.'

'I don't know what to say.'

'I don't know what to do.'

That's what the hole was for.

It is easy to get carried along by the flow. It doesn't matter what sort of flow it is. Water, wine, conversation, the rhythm of digging, poetry. We are predisposed to be carried along, if we are like Martin. Stepping into any sort of flow is dangerous for us, if we are like Martin. And if, like Martin, at some unexpected bend, or shallows, or falls, we find ourselves cast ashore, it is almost instinctive to step in again, to find some other flow of which to make ourselves a part. We are comfortable, being carried along. Carried by those around us, by our own illusions, needs, desperations.

'It won't do.' Robert said.

'That doesn't help.'

'I know.'

'At least you've stopped digging.'

'Which is what everyone says you should do.'

'When you're in a hole.'

'But then what?'

'Then you climb out.'

Martin was sitting in the hole. He was wearing a long coat wrapped around his knees, which he had drawn up so that he could hold them close against himself with his clasped hands. He was wearing a black micro-fibre hat, pulled down at the back over his ears, making the top of his head look very round. His shoes, which poked out from under the hem of the coat, were caked in clay, wet clay beneath which a crusting of earlier, dried out clay, showed as a paler colour. Streaks of rust brown colour marked his face. His hair was matted with it, like the hair of someone who has suffered a serious head injury.

'I can't do that.'

'You must.'

The spade was planted in the earth beside the hole, not in it. A dewdrop of silver grey sky hung from the handgrip. Robert pulled it clear and hefted it in his hands. He had not held a spade for years. It was lighter than he remembered. He shook it, like a native in an old movie, shaking a spear. Martin closed his eyes.

'Huh! Huh! Huh!'

With each spade-full Robert grunted, just as Martin had done. He worked from the side nearest to him. The clay was softer than he had expected, but it was still heavy. It clung to the blade, as if it did not want to be put back into the hole. He threw it, jerking the spade back at the far reach of his arms to detach the heavy clods. They fell with a thump against Martin's boots, against his legs. Martin did not open his eyes. He did not move. He did not cry out. Robert continued to dig, and throw. Huh! Huh! Huh! Martin's feet vanished beneath the glistening mound. Robert worked deeper into the curving slope. The clay piled against Martin's thighs, against his buttocks.

Jane went up to the bathroom and took off her blouse. She did not draw the blinds but looked out of the window, down to the orchard to where she could see Robert's head and shoulders moving rhythmically as those might of a man making love slowly, relentlessly, against an unresisting partner. She slipped out of her jeans and hung them over the towel rail. She peeled down her tights and knickers, disentangled them and discarded them in the laundry basket. Then she reached around behind her shoulders and unclipped the white bra and threw that too into the basket.

Then, having taken one more glance out of the window, she turned to the shower, switched it on, and having waited a second or two for the cold water to clear from the pipe, stepped in under the cascade.

Just before he covered the head, working now from the other side of the slope Robert saw Martin briefly open his eyes. Neither of them said anything. Martin made no noise. He did not move at all. Robert carried on digging. That was the difference, he thought, between being in a hole, and out of one, not stopping digging. He was surprised how difficult it was to fill the hole, even after Martin had disappeared entirely from view. He worked on into the night, deciding in the end, to break down the overhanging lip of turf above and to the sides. When he had finished there was still a small depression, as if there had been some minor underground subsidence such as was common once in coal mining areas when the pit-roads were only a few feet below the surface. That was odd, he thought, considering that Martin lay below. The thought then struck him that when graves were dug they were always left mounded up, so that as the body decayed, and the coffin, the ground would settle to its original level. He looked around the trampled clay. There was no way that he could scrape up enough of it here to make such a mound, not tonight anyway.

Dawn was already showing on the eastern horizon when he went in. I suppose it is superfluous to mention eastern, that being the only horizon over which the dawn could show, but it locates us here, rather than on some counter-spinning planet of cosmic fiction. Of course, even such an invented place might have an eastern horizon. Perhaps we are not so firmly located then, after all.

Jane was waiting for him. She was wearing new undergarments that she had been saving. She stripped his clothes from him in the kitchen, and with her finger to her lips led him naked past the bedroom where Merle lay sleeping. When he had showered and dried himself, she took him into her own room.

Out in the orchard, for a while, Martin, or perhaps it was the wind, howled.

That was all there was to it, but we have time to spare. We have words to spare. Do you have questions? I will answer them if I can. Martin? Martin, like all men was essentially useless. Like all men, it took Martin some time to understand this, but, like all men, he did so in the end, and having come to that understanding what was he confronted with? Without use. He could have made himself useful perhaps. He could have told a story to pass the time, this story even. Yet time passes anyway. It needs no help from Martin, or from other men, to pass. He could have run errands, done small jobs. His parents, often enough, had told him, 'Make yourself useful Martin,' although they had never specified to whom, or how. He had assumed always that it was to them. Yet his parents were fifty percent useless themselves, one of them being like Martin and all other men. In fact Martin's usefulness would only have been a sham.

All this was true of Robert too. Only Jane could save them, and even she could not make them useful, essentially. There was nothing that they could do that could not have been done by other means, among her women friends, and with less angst, less disappointment. Jane was complicit in the hiding of their uselessness. Martin found out the truth sooner. That was all.

What else would you like to know?

Did they get away with it? Of course not. None of them did. Not even Merle, and she was guilty of nothing. The ground, as if it regretted how it had pinioned him while he died, rolled and fought against his corpse, rejected it, pushed it upwards, expelled it. The smell of his rotting hung beneath the apple trees and tainted their fruit. Flies bred in him and flew out through fissures in the clay, swarms of them, buzzing. They vomited Martin onto the skins of the apples and ate him again, sweetened with fruit.

In the end Robert went away. He could not bring himself to dig another hole, but walked out, stepping into the path of the oncoming road, and letting it carry him away to oblivion. Jane could not stop him, but she watched, from the upstairs window, naked, with her fine undergarments washed and laid out upon the bed, in case he should return.

Some people tell you that all you need is food, and shelter, and warm clothing, and work, but none of these things is of any use to the useless. You might as well dig a hole, and sit down in it, and wait for someone who understands to come along and fill it in over your head, not a comfortable hole, but one filled with ends of worms, and an oozy smell.

Poem For The Love Lane Crow

Gareth Durasow

This is the way of an adulteress:
she eats, and wipes her mouth,
and says, 'I have done no wrong.'
- Proverbs 30:20

Sheba contemplates the kill:
inkblot no. 5 with satin tines unfurled.
Deciding that it will just have to do
she unravels its best laid plans of guts
like a skein of wool across the grass
till light enough for lugging up
brickwork inclines so sheer that
Sisyphus, this near to suicide,
regards his granite albatross
a stone's throw from a lark
and Jacob Marley perseveres
inside that genius locksmith's wet dream,
grateful that at least his burden doesn't bleed.

No belfry rings for the crow,
just the bell for summoning serfs
as Sheba explodes in a fission of math,
her calculations breaking terraces down
to their elementary stone step flights.
She shuns the limelight indulging the strays
applauded by the doors of bleak estates,
returns to the yard she's anointed with piss
where Koi carp still can't make their heckles heard.

Sheba reclining and bibbed in blood
considers how best to exhibit the kill
now sodden and grey, the black having run
like print in a bible brought in from the rain.

Stinky

Ben Cheetham

The smell is almost impossible to describe. Have you ever caught a whiff of the juice that collects at the bottom of a bin when people don't bag their rubbish? My dad, who worked as a binman for twenty years, calls it maggot juice. Well it's a bit like that, only much, much worse. Worse, in fact, than anything you could imagine.

A couple of days ago I asked my wife, Polly, if she could smell it. She gave me a puzzled look. 'Smell what?'

'You mean you honestly can't smell it?'

'I don't even know what you're talking about, Mark.'

I was reassured, but that didn't stop me from rushing out to stock up on soap and deodorant. I spent the best part of an hour in the shower. It didn't get rid of the smell, though.

'You're not starting with all that again, are you?' said Polly.

I avoided eye contact with her.

The next day I was over an hour late for work. I lied to my manager that my car had broken down.

'Are you alright?' He asked. 'You look a little pale.'

It's the stink, I wanted to reply, it's making me feel sick. Mumbling something about not having slept very well, I hurried away to my desk.

I didn't get much work done over the next couple of hours. It's hard to concentrate when you're fighting an urge to vomit. Eventually, it got so bad I was forced to make a dash for the toilets. After washing my mouth out with liquid soap and spraying a full can of deodorant over myself, I felt able to return to my desk. Then, to my horror, somebody said, 'Christ, what's that smell?'

My panic was instantaneous and overwhelming. It picked me up and sent me running for the stairwell. It didn't loosen its grip until I was in my car driving fast with all the windows wound down.

I showered five times that afternoon. By the time Polly got in from work along with our son Charlie, who attends a day nursery, my skin was red raw and bleeding in places.

'It's back,' I said.

A weary look came into Polly's face. 'Why?'

'I don't know,' I lied.

'Something must've triggered it.' As I turned my eyes to the floor, Polly added, 'Don't do that. Speak to me.'

She said something else, but I wasn't listening to her anymore. I was thinking about the newspaper article I'd been carrying around in my pocket for the last couple of days, picturing Valda Hanratty's face. The brown hair was thinner and greyer, the eyes were dimmer, the mouth was even more downturned, but it was still unmistakably her. My insides had turned to ice when I saw her staring at me from under the headline, '27 years after schoolboy went missing, mother still hoping someone will come forward and say what happened to him.'

'Where are you going?' Polly asked when I walked past her suddenly.

I made no reply.

* * *

'Watch out, here comes Stinky,' the other kids in my class used to whisper when they saw me. Some of them would hold their noses or pretend to gag. Others would gag for real, especially if it was a hot day.

Our teacher, Mrs Beckingham, always smiled sympathetically at me, but I could tell from her face that even she was repulsed by my body odour.

All the kids sat two or three to a table, except for me. No one, not even the Gypsy kids who sometimes attended the school for stints of six months or a year, would sit next to me.

In the classroom the name-calling was mostly restricted to whispers, but in the playground the other kids would yell, 'Get lost, Stinky, we don't want to catch your germs.'

It's not my fault, I wanted to yell back at them, I wash every

day the same as you do, it's just that I've got this problem.
I knew it wouldn't have made any difference though, other than perhaps marking me out as even more of a freak.

Name-calling wasn't the worst of what I had to put up with either. There was spitting, punching, kicking, stone-throwing and a good deal else besides.

'You've got to learn to stick up for yourself, Mark,' was mum's standard response when I returned home with a bloodied nose or split lip, which was more often than not.

She meant well, I know, but as I found out to my cost her advice was worse than useless.

* * *

I was twenty years old, unemployed and living as a virtual recluse when I was diagnosed as suffering from fish odour syndrome. The bad news was that there was no cure. The good news was that it could be kept under control by avoiding certain foods.
I started on a strict diet and within a matter of weeks the smell of rotting fish that had clung to me like a curse since I was nine months old was gone. To say I was relieved would be an understatement. As far as I was concerned, it was a miracle.

I quickly got a job and, to everyone's surprise, including my own, a girlfriend. Neither lasted very long, but it didn't matter, there would be more jobs and lots more girlfriends. After years of stagnating, things were suddenly moving so fast I hardly gave the past a thought, that is until I got a job in the same office as Simon Pratley.

The job was a dream come true for me. I'd spent the bulk of my teenage years locked away in my bedroom with only a computer for company. Now I was going to be training as a computer programmer. On my first day, as I was being shown around the office, a loud voice called out, 'Hey, Stinky.'

I recognised my tormentor-in-chief from school instantly, although he was taller, stockier and balder than when I'd last seen him. A wave of dizziness rose in me as he approached with a familiar arrogant grin on his face. He jutted his chin toward me, sniffing.

'I don't smell bad anymore,' I stammered.

'Thank Christ for that.' He extended a hand, but withdrew it quickly when I made to shake it. 'Whoa, I don't want to catch any germs.'

I stared at him, speechless and near panic. Laughing, he grabbed my hand and squeezed hard. 'Only joking, mate. Welcome to Logic Programming Associates.'

* * *

Simon Pratley was shaving well before I hit puberty. At fourteen I wasn't short for my age, but he was a good seven inches taller than me and far more solidly built. For some reason that no one could understand, he was best mates with a sour-faced runt named Jamie Hanratty. They made an odd couple – the overgrown bully and his pigeon-chested sidekick. But nobody dared laugh at them.

Without Pratley, Jamie Hanratty was just another spiteful little no mark. With him, he was one of the most hated boys in school and a glance from his small shrewd eyes was enough to make you tremble in your boots.

It was Hanratty who first called me Stinky. We were eight years old. He was new at school. I decided to try and make friends with him, but when I approached him he made a disgusted face and yelled, 'Go away Stinky.'

Some of the other kids found my new nickname so amusing that they chased me around the playground holding their noses whilst chanting it. From that day onward practically the only people at school who called me Mark were my teachers.

Over the next six years, as the bullying continued relentlessly, I withdrew more and more into myself, nurturing a sense of rage and injustice. By the time I turned fourteen things had got so bad that I often refused to speak to anyone, my parents included, for days at a time.

It was dad's idea to get the puppy. He said it would be good for me to have a little responsibility. The puppy was a chocolate-brown Labrador called Joe. It was my job to feed and walk him every afternoon.

My favourite walk was alongside a canal not far from our house. The towpath was usually deserted and if I did bump into anybody the rank smell given off by the scum that collected on the water's surface would mask my B.O. After about half a mile there was a tunnel whose entrance was overshadowed by an oak tree. It was there that I ran into Hanratty and his crew. I should have turned for home as soon as I saw them, but instead I ducked behind a bush and watched them play. A jolt of longing for a world I'd never known shot through me as Hanratty swung over the water on a rope-swing they'd set up.

Suddenly, Joe yanked the lead out of my grasp and raced toward the boys. As I started after him, Pratley called out, 'Hey, it's Stinky.'

Hanratty picked up Joe by the scruff of his neck.

'Give him here or –' I began in a scared, but defiantly loud voice.

'Or what?' interrupted Hanratty, grinning.

I made a grab for Joe, but Pratley caught my wrist and twisted it behind my back. 'What shall we do with him?' he said.

A malicious gleam came into Hanratty's eyes. 'I know, let's give him a bath.'

Him and another boy grabbed one of my legs each and hoisted me off my feet. 'Please don't,' I begged as they swung me over the water.

'On three,' said Hanratty. Then he began to count. They released me with a whoop. I landed on my back several feet out in the channel. Scummy water rushed up my nostrils. I came to the surface retching from the taste of it.

'Help,' I gasped, flailing about desperately as my feet sank into a thick sludge.

Hanratty and his cronies were rolling around in fits of laughter. He tossed Joe into the water and, along with the other boys, ran into the tunnel.

The sludge sucked my trainers off as, clutching Joe to my chest, I thrashed my way to the edge of the canal. I collapsed onto my back wheezing like an asthmatic. There was a strange buzzing sensation in my head. My vision began to blur.

Even now I can't say for certain what happened next. I

vaguely remember Joe whining and struggling to get free. Then I must have blacked out briefly, because the next thing I knew I was waking up and he was silent and still. It was obvious at once that he was dead. Horrified and confused, I ran home cradling him in my arms.

'How did this happen?' asked dad.

'He jumped into the canal,' I lied. 'I went in after him, but he'd already drowned.'

What was I supposed to say? That I'd strangled him to death, only I couldn't remember doing it. They'd have put me in a loony-bin and thrown away the key.

* * *

I had my second nervous breakdown not long after starting work at Logic Programming Associates. I should have quit as soon as I discovered that Simon Pratley worked there, but I kept telling myself I could handle it. I was wrong.

I'd been there for a couple of months, getting on alright, when Pratley came over to my desk and said, 'You know what today is, don't you?'

I pretended not to hear him, hoping he'd go away.

'It's seven years exactly since Jamie disappeared.'

My body went rigid. There was a tingling in my brain, which intensified as Pratley went on, 'It's stupid I know, but I still believe that one day he might turn up alive. What do you think?'

In a slow, barely audible voice I told him that I didn't know.

That evening I noticed the smell for the first time. It was unlike anything I'd ever smelt before, but it was what I imagined a decomposing body to smell like.

'Can you smell that?' I asked mum.

'Smell what?' she replied.

By the following morning the smell had got so bad that it made me nauseous. Again and again I asked mum if she could smell it and got the same, increasingly exasperated reply. I knew she was right, but I doubted my perception.

From then on my health deteriorated fast. I could hardly bring myself to eat. I'd always been a borderline obsessive when it came to personal hygiene, but now I was spending six or seven hours a day in the bathroom. I would have ended up in hospital for certain, if it hadn't been for Polly.

At the time I'd been seeing her casually for several months, so it came as no surprise when she showed up at the house asking to see me. What did come as a surprise was the way she refused to take no for an answer. God knows why, but day after day she came knocking until I reluctantly told mum to let her in.

'Are you ill?' she asked.

'No.'

'What's wrong with you then?'

'I don't know.'

She tried to take my hand, but I flinched away from her. I had a vague notion that my touch would contaminate her in some way. There were tears in her eyes as she stood to leave.

'Is it alright if I come to see you tomorrow?' she asked.

'Do as you please,' I replied as if I wasn't bothered. Inwardly, though, I was terrified she wouldn't come again. I realised my fear was needless when she looked at me with that deep understanding she has.

Over the next few weeks Polly visited me every day. She had a gentle but effective way of finding out what she wanted to know. Gradually, I opened up and told her pretty much the entire story of how fish odour syndrome had ruined the first twenty years of my life and how my greatest fear was that it would return to ruin the rest of it. I never talked about Joe, though, or about what happened on the day Jamie Hanratty went missing. How do you tell someone you love that kind of thing?

* * *

The last time Valda Hanratty saw Jamie he was heading out to meet up with his friends. He was wearing white trainers, blue polyester tracksuit bottoms, a grey-and-black striped T-shirt and a blue hooded jacket with a catapult in one of its pockets. She didn't know about the catapult.

When Jamie didn't return for his dinner, she rang around his friends and learned that he hadn't met up with them as planned. She waited another two hours before contacting the police.

A search of the surrounding neighbourhood and wooded areas was quickly got under way. Sex offenders living in the area were questioned. An appeal was made to the public for information. The canal was dredged. All to no avail. Jamie Hanratty, it seemed, had literally vanished into thin air.

Day by day any hope of finding him alive faded. After a couple of months everyone had accepted that there was virtually no chance of him turning up alive. Everyone that is except Valda Hanratty.

It said in the paper that unless someone could prove otherwise, she would go to her grave refusing to believe her son was dead. She even intended to leave her house to a relative on the condition that when Jamie came home they handed it over to him. That's what finally decided it for me. Enough is enough, I said to myself.

* * *

'You should give Dr Lewis a call,' said Polly.

'It wouldn't do any good.'

'He's helped you in the past.'

There's no therapist in the world who can help me now I wanted to reply, but instead I turned to Charlie and said, 'Daddy's got to go now. I want you to be a good boy for your mum while I'm gone.'

Charlie made an indignant face. 'I'm always a good boy, daddy.'

I was careful not to touch him or Polly as I stood to leave.

'Where are you going?' she asked.

'Nowhere in particular. I'll be back soon.'

What a stinking coward I am, I kept thinking as I drove to my parent's house. Even when it's too late to make any real difference, I can't bring myself to tell the only person who's ever understood me the truth face-to-face.

I parked in the drive, made my way to the potting-shed in the back garden, removed a section of slatted wooden flooring and began digging up its earthen base with a spade.

About four feet down, the spade crunched through a yellowish-brown, hollow bone. I dropped to my knees and continued digging with my hands. When the entire skeleton was exposed, I carefully transferred it to a bag and set off on the short walk to Valda Hanratty's house.

I hurried past the spot where twenty seven years earlier I'd collapsed in agony when Jamie Hanratty shot me in the stomach with his catapult. I remember him standing over me laughing. After that there's a blank space in my memory. All I know is that when I did come to, I wished I hadn't.

A familiar looking boy, perhaps eight years old, answered the door of Valda Hanratty's house.

'Is your grandma in?' I asked.

'Who are you?'

'My name's Stinky.'

The boy giggled. 'That's a silly name.'

'I know.' I smiled at him. 'Run and fetch your grandma.'

'What shall I tell her?'

'Tell her...' My voice faltered. For a moment I thought I was going to fall over, but the feeling passed and my voice was quite level as I said, 'Tell her Jamie's come home.'

The Flight Of Swallows

Kate Dempsey

A single swallow flies somehow
in the window, the gap she comes through

as thick as your hospital chart,
realises her mistake and skirts

the stitched screen, wheels, her wing an inch
from the ceiling and speeds once, twice

slap bang into the pane. I, standing
one boot on, one off, fluttering

as useless as when they restrained
you to deliver insulin,

the thin needles made you cry;
you held my wrist fast, as tight

as when your fist first grasped my hand.
She thumps into the glass again;

a clump of grey breast-down floats
to the floor. And she's flown so far

from that baked Sahara fringe,
to this cold north; all so pointless – breaking

on my frayed-sash window. And me,
my mouth again a soundless O.

I flap forward with one bare foot
to force the window perhaps or scoot

her out – there must be something I could
do. If I could take your place, I would.

She swoops around with one last sweep
of her tail, skims the ledge and escapes.

Song Thrush

Jacquie Shanahan

You brought me the shovel, a piece of slate,
I scraped up a bracelet of flies,
a hairnet of feathers, sheer weight-
lessness. You covered your eyes.
I marched her past the ripening pears,
exhaling the smell of glue, and you
pressed your fingers into your ears
as though songs could kill you too.
We buried her deep in the dry stone wall,
a cave for her echoes, slow rise, quick fall.

The Door

Helen Simpson

Organising a new back door after the break-in was more complicated than you might imagine. Even sourcing a ready-made door to fit the existing frame took some doing. After following a couple of false trails I drove to a little DIY shop five miles away, in a draughty row of shops just off the A3 after the Tolworth Tower turning.

Bleak from outside, this charmless parade supplied all sorts of seductive and useful items when you looked more closely. Under the dustbin lid of a sky were: a travel agent offering cut-price controlled escapes; a newsagent with a bank of magazine smiles on entry and a surprisingly choice collection of sweets (real Turkish Delight, macadamia praline, Alpine milk chocolate); an art shop with dusty sleeping cat at the foot of a good wooden easel; a cafe with formica tables, a constant frying pan and a big steel teapot. If you looked closely and in the right way, all the pleasures and comforts were accessible here in this dogleg just off the Tolworth turning, as well as all the nuts and bolts. It was the first time for months that I'd been able to entertain such a thought. In the iron light of February I entered the hardware shop and inside was a little community of goodwill and respect.

The woman on the other side of the counter listened to me attentively, looked at me with kind eyes from behind her glasses, and explained the sizes, finishes, charges and extras for the various models of ready-made doors they could supply. While she did this she also dealt with a couple of phone calls, politely and efficiently, and paused for a few seconds to admire the baby asleep in the arms of the cafe owner from next door who had come round with some query about his ceiling, promising herself aloud a cuddle once my order had been taken. Since the seventeenth of August I had grown unimaginative about others, selfishly incurious and sometimes downright hostile. Now, here, some sort of thaw was taking place. A tall man in overalls was talking to the shop's manager, telling him about the progress of a job out in West Molesey, and it seemed it was going well.

There was an atmosphere of good temper which was rare and warming, none of the usual sighs or in-staff carping or reined-in impatience when you wanted to know how much it would be with extra safety bolts or with three coats of paint rather than two. I was charmed. I wanted to stay in this dim toasty light amid the general friendliness and walls festooned with hosepipes, tubes of grouting and sealant, boxes of thumbtacks, lightbulbs, my mind soothed by the industrious but not frantic atmosphere.

Everything here had to do with maintenance and soundness. Grief kept indoors grows noxious, I thought, like a room that can't be aired; mould grows, plants die. I wanted to open the windows but it wasn't allowed.

The order was complicated – did I want full or partial beading, what about a weatherboard, the door furniture, would I prefer a silver or gold finish, or perhaps this brushed aluminium – and it took quite a while. Even so, I was sorry when it was finished and Sally – the young woman's name – had handed me my carbon copy and swiped a hundred pounds from my Barclaycard as the deposit. Because even a very ordinary ready-made back door was going to cost £400 in total to supply, fit, hang and paint.

'They're not cheap, are they, doors,' I said, as I signed the slip.

'They're not,' she sighed in agreement, not taking my comment in any way personally. 'But they're well-made, these doors. Nice and strong.'

'Good,' I said, tucking the Visa slip into my wallet. For a moment I toyed with the idea of telling her how they'd kicked the last one in, but I couldn't face the effort. Even so I felt she was like a sister to me.

'So Matthew will be along on the twenty-second to hang the door and paint it,' she said.

'You've got my number in case he needs to change the date.'

'Yes, that's right, but expect him on the twenty-second at

about nine-thirty,' she said. 'Matthew is very dependable.'

* * *

At nine thirty-five on the twenty-second I had a phone call, and I relaxed at the sound of Sally's calm voice, even though I was expecting her to cancel the door-fitting appointment with all the irritation that would involve. I had with difficulty arranged a day at home to deal with a couple of files from the office, without having to take it off my annual holiday allowance. But she was not ringing to cancel, no, she was only ringing to let me know that the traffic was terrible that morning and Matthew had rung her to say he was stuck out in a jam near Esher but should be with me before ten.

He arrived at two minutes to, the tall man in overalls I had seen earlier in the shop; he had a frank open face and unforced smile. As he walked into the kitchen at the back my shoulders dropped and I gave a sigh as thorough as a baby's yawn. It was going to be all right.

'Would you like tea or coffee?' I asked, raising the kettle to show this was no idle offer.

'Not just now, thank you,' he said. 'Later would be good, but I'd better get cracking on straight away.'

Again he smiled that nice natural smile. He was not going to be chatty, how wonderful, I would be able to trust him and leave him to it and get on with my work. He did not need respectful hovering attendance as the man who had recently mended the boiler had done; nor me running around for step ladders and spare bits and pieces that he might have forgotten, like the electrician before Christmas just after I'd moved in. That had been three months after the funeral I wasn't at. First I'd chucked things out in a sort of frenzy, binbags to Oxfam, but then I'd realised that wouldn't be enough, I'd have to move. Which I'd done, somehow.

I hovered around a bit while he brought in his toolboxes. Then, staggering only slightly and with a shallow stertorousness of breathing and blossom of sweat on his forehead, he carried in the door itself, a raw glazed slab of timber that looked too narrow for the destined frame.

'I didn't quite realise...' I said. 'I thought it was going to be ready painted, ready to hang today.'

'It is ready to hang,' he said. 'But first I must see how it fits, I must shave anywhere it's a bit tight. I must see wherever it needs adjusting to the frame.'

'Oh, so it's not just standard; I see,' I said.

'The frame is a standard size from the measurements you took, but they're always a few centimetres out here and there,' he explained. He wasn't irritated or bored by my questions, but at the same time he continued to prepare for work, spreading a groundsheet, setting out his tools.

'We want a perfect fit,' he said, looking up, looking me in the eye. 'But don't worry, it'll all be done by the end of today.'

I hardly ever believe a man when he says that sort of thing, but this one I did. I went into the front room and sat down to work. The disabling sluggishness which had dogged me ever since I'd moved here, stagnant as my reflection in the mirror, seemed to have beaten a temporary retreat. It was over two hours before I looked up again, though I had been distantly aware of the sounds of drilling and tapping, finding them reassuring rather than distracting. There was satisfaction in two people working separately but companionably in the flat. It was dignified.

I went through to the kitchen.

'Are you ready for a coffee now?' I asked. 'It's nearly twelve-thirty. I'll be making myself a sandwich, shall I do one for you too? Just cheese and tomato.'

I hadn't cooked anything in this kitchen. Nuts and raisins, toast, that was about it. I really couldn't be bothered.

'I'll say yes to the coffee and no to the sandwich,' he said, looking briefly in my direction, his concentration needed for the door, which he appeared to have in a wrestling hold half way into the frame. 'Thank you.'

'Can I help?' I said feebly, despising myself immediately for putting him under the necessity of making a polite refusal while struggling with a seven foot door. The wood was still in its patchy undercoat. Outside, the air was the opposite of crisp, and chill with it.

'Not brilliant painting weather,' I commented as I sawed away at the loaf.

'I don't think it'll rain quite yet,' he said. 'Not till the evening. And the paint should have gone off by then. You'll know when it's gone off, when you're safe, by licking your finger and then just touching the surface of the gloss. If it's smooth, you're safe. If it's still tacky you'll have to wait a bit longer.'

Safe – that word – I thought I'd never hear it again. And of course there is no safety but it's nice to hear it spoken of.

'Will you really have time to give it two coats?' I said. 'What happens after you've applied the first one?'

'Then I have to be a bit patient but it doesn't take as long as you'd think,' he said, at work now on lining up the hinges with the places marked for them on the frame.

'Watching paint dry,' I suggested, and smiled.

I felt better than I had for weeks, I'd worked hard and happily this morning and would continue to do so after my sandwich, with him round the corner. I saw what a ghost I'd become in these rooms, invisible, restless, talking to myself and leaving half-finished sentences in the air.

He had a row of little brass screws held by the line of his lips, like a seamstress with her mouthful of pins, and frowned as he prepared the path for the first of them with the tip of a bradawl. I put his coffee on the draining board beside him, then perched on a kitchen stool over by the breadbin while I ate my sandwich. The hinges went on well and without trouble. He stood up at last and straightened his back.

'That's more like it,' he said, and picked up the mug of coffee.

'It looks lovely,' I said truthfully. 'The last one was too old, I think, the wood was rotten in the corner and really it wouldn't have kept a squirrel out if it was determined. Let alone a burglar.'

'You had a break-in then,' he said, shaking his head.

'Opportunistic the police said when they came round,' I replied, remembering the two young boys with their notebooks and curt chivalry. One of them had had a large fading bruise on his cheekbone.

'I've got a couple of good sliding bolts to fit on this door,' he said, 'that and the Chubb lock mean that things should be as secure as they can be.'

'Excellent,' I said.

I wanted to tell him, that meant nothing. Out of the blue your heart can stop beating and you're dead. All finished in twenty minutes. No warning. Nothing. I'd finished my sandwich.

I should go back to the front room table now and make a start on the next file, but somehow I felt like loitering in the kitchen.

'Funny how things come all at the same time,' I continued. The business of trying to utter natural words from the heart, frank and clear, struck me with dismal force, the inevitable difficulty involved in discovering ourselves to others, the clichés and blindness and inadvertent misrepresentations, but I thought I would have a go anyway.

'Yes, all sorts of things,' I said, but I suddenly couldn't be bothered to mention personal details. One step at a time. One day at a time. Yeah, yeah.

'You just have to put your head down and keep walking, sometimes,' I blurted. 'Keep on keeping on. Never mind the weather.'

He nodded and sipped his coffee. He didn't think I was mad. I wasn't mad, but I was very shaken, very shuddery inside when I remembered things. My mind had been behaving like a bonfire, feed it a dry and crackling little worry and it would leap into flame.

'I know what you mean,' he said. 'When something happens. Takes over. I've had a few weeks when it's been hard to think of anything else. Well, me and my wife both, really.'

He paused, took another sip of coffee.

'These friends of ours,' he continued, 'A month ago, their flat caught fire, they lived above a garage, it was the wiring, and they lost their two youngest. In the fire. It was in the papers.'

'Oh God,' I groaned. 'How terrible.' My eyes were filling up, my throat had a rock halfway down.

'We've been trying to help see them through it,' he said. 'But there's not much you can say.'

'No,' I said.

'You can be there, though,' he added, turning back to the

door.

'You have to watch it, pity,' I said in a rush. 'Pity could finish you off.'

'That's right,' he said. 'In the end you have to say to yourself, no I'm not going to think about that for now. We had to do that, me and my wife, we weren't getting to sleep at night.'

'Because it doesn't help anyone in the end,' I snorted. 'If you go under yourself then you certainly won't be able to hold out a strong hand to help.'

'That's right,' he said again, and his smile was full of honesty and warmth.

I wondered what his wife was like, whether she was equally generous-natured. My dead love had been married, married with a vengeance though he'd never shown me her photo.

'I must get back to my files,' I said.

'And I can start on the painting now,' he replied, glancing anxiously at the sky.

I had another restorative work session, concentrating well and thoroughly absorbed. Thank God for work. Save us from the obsessive mental mill which constantly grinds but never digests. Secrecy doesn't come naturally to me, and this enforced silence was a punishment for which even his wronged wife might have pitied me, had she known about me. For the first time I wondered what she was going through, wherever she was. Later in the afternoon, Matthew called to me from the kitchen that I should come and have a look.

The door was glossy with its second white coat, immaculate. It had two silver bolts, which he demonstrated would slide easily and slickly into the plates he'd fitted in the frame, and along with the Chubb lock these two would make the door trebly secure. He handed me the small silver key which would fasten them in place, and the larger one for the Chubb, which was gold in colour.

'Better not shut it for another couple of hours,' he suggested. 'With luck the rain'll hold off that long; I think it will, but if you shut it before then the paint won't have hardened enough, it'll stick to the frame when you shut it then rip away and leave raw wood when you open it again. So leave it to harden for as long as you can before you shut the door.'

I can recognise good advice when I hear it. This was what I'd needed to know.

'Thank you,' I said. 'Thank you.'

Thin Red Line

Lynn Roberts

They diminish their corner of the pub.
Too large, too loud, too many legs – too long –
weaving the dolls' oak table with its clutch
of foam-mapped glasses; arms straining
their T-shirt sleeves like saveloys. The wine-
drinkers shift, flick glances, crimp their brows
under the cannonades of laughter, plosive words,
jokes with the pin pulled out tossed round the bar,
and turn their backs and fidget, heave and sigh.

Then, somehow, we're aware of who these are –
that they've come home, but will be going out
                            again

to dusty televised townships we can
barely imagine, where each corner,
every car, each coat's a threat; and where
keeping your silence keeps your life; where arms
by default go with the man; where legs
draw clouds of metal midges; where men wait
with dread like a silver fish leaping the throat
for the world to part in a red wound
and death to fly out like a
                         full stop.

The View From Darwin Gardens

Jim Greenhalf

Rain clouds rumble over Hebers Ghyll,
Panorama Rocks and Weary Hill,
pelting fur and feather along Pancake Ridge;
strafing Jags and Mercs on Curly Hill
across the Victorian river bridge.
A fanfare of late summer sunshine
summons spinsters and widows to tiffin
from privately-wooded thoroughfares.
In Betty's they're fortified with Earl Grey,
Darjeeling and upholstered éclairs.
The green detonations of Middleton Wood.
Under those broccoli bunches, flowers
parade in uniform shades of blue.
From khaki to Roman bronze and amber,
the pebble-dashing river changes hue.

Rushmore sculptures shape the air,
as the night trains recruit males
with cocky coxcombs, tattoos
and private hurts to quench.
Tonight they'll snatch relief in booze
and girls. Tomorrow, those old enough to die
for bluebells, Betty's and folk on Curly Hill,
will be cock of the Wharfe no more.
They fly them out on Pegasus,
boys apprenticed to be men of war;
eyes brighter than summer at Robin Hood's Bay.
They will send them back in Union Jack
boxes, to Brize Norton or Lynam;
and at the going down of the sun
we will remember them – but not for long.

A Dangerous Crossing

Penny Aldred

Skala Bay. A few minutes south of the town, where boys go to meet boys and old men like me sometimes get lucky. In the afternoon they're there, these young men, playing football. They wear Bermuda shorts and shades, rush into each other, thighs pressing across thighs to reach the ball, arms round waists to steady themselves, eyes catching eyes as they arrange to rendezvous later. Holiday makers, not islanders like me. Young men arriving on charter flights from England and Germany.

I often walk down after lunch, sit at one of the cafés, not right by that beach, their beach but one the other side of the bay, a discreet, questionable distance away. Drink a coffee, an ouzo, watch the horizon, the cruise ships far away that miss this island, and study the boys. Running beads through my fingers. I'm not the only one making casual glances to the football. There are three or four others, in their forties and fifties. Me, I've still a couple of years to forty. Not so old really you see. But it feels as though I am. Old and too late. Though I had a chance once, of love.

In the village in the hills where I was raised, my family have reared sheep and grown olives for ever, and his have grown vines and fermented wine. I remember glances across a table as the village celebrated the harvest gathered. Later and alone, with his hand in the small of my back, we climbed over sunwashed rocks to the afternoon song of the cicadas. For our night time encounters when the village slept we followed the same steps, lit by the moon, and lay together far from the village. My family bought a new olive press. There was another party, our arms round shoulders as men could, and a photo, us leaning too close, so right together. It told who we were and I hated it.

He'd have tried a life together there, but not me. Nor would

I leave for another island, bigger, more anonymous. He felt I was choosing family over him, never knew it was cowardice over bravery, lies over truth. In the end he went without me, first to Crete, and then Athens. I stayed and lived the lie.

In the hills, I've sometimes seen Nikos, when he's been over for a visit, growing smarter city slick by the year. In the twenty years since we've parted I've tried to avoid meeting him, avoided being at a celebration together or where it was not possible, I've ignored him. One winter, God help me, I paid particular attention to Eleni, a young woman from the next village. Time was pressing for her if she wasn't to remain single and I gave her hopes. She wasted four or five months on me when she should have been watching the man who'd taken over a derelict farmhouse, made it into a pottery. He clearly needed a wife and had taken a fancy to her. Too late he married someone else. And Nikos, in the couple of visits he made that winter, I saw him watching me, me with Eleni, puzzled.

Life was empty without him. I had too much time alone, to think. Shaking the olive trees to drop them into black nets, loading them into baskets, working the press didn't occupy my thoughts enough. I needed distractions to forget what had passed and not ponder on tomorrow. Stretching empty ahead.

So when tourists started coming to the island, for the sun, cheap food and wine it was a chance for me to spend the summers away. Now April to September I live by the sea, the mornings delivering bread to the hotels in and around the town, and in the evening I work in a wine bar. I go back to the village when the season is over. The coast here is abandoned, the apartments and restaurants boarded up. Just a few old folk who were here before the tourists, and the cats, scavenging through the winter months.

There are turtles breeding a couple of kilometres from the town. When they were first found it looked like the boom was over and I'd be back at the village full time. Some academic came from the university in Athens and asked questions about the damage the tourists were doing in the breeding season, the noise, the bright lights, the beach full of bodies catching the sun.

He spent a season watching what was going on. There were

meetings with the shopkeepers, the hoteliers and then it was all on again, but controlled. With posters urging everyone to take care, mind the breeding sites, don't frighten the turtles, this is their home. The shops sell videos in high season, telling the story of the turtles. They sell postcards, enamel brooches, turtle images woven into rugs. Volunteers come from abroad and work with Greek students to help protect the turtles, to find a way for them to survive alongside the tourists. There is a small building, it used to be a wash house. It's been rebuilt and the walls whitewashed, now it's a museum. There are long stretches of sand where the tourists can go. On the turtles' beach there are bamboo sticks marked with flags to show where the breeding site is, to stop people playing volleyball or setting up picnics where the new turtles are trying to cross the sand. So we get tourists here who like the turtles and are interested in our plants and animals. They can be seen climbing up through the olive groves, heading for the hills with their binoculars, or crouched down watching the lizards sunbathing on the house walls.

Then, four or five years ago, another kind of tourist arrived, men who liked men. I was drawn to the bay by my memories of Nikos.

So now by the sea I spend the afternoons watching the football, avoiding the eyes of the others who are too scared. They are probably like me, allowing a young man into their beds, occasionally and fearfully. I'm reduced to taking the image of those boys home to my room above the baker's, to my solitary bed. Remembering their skin, smooth, youthful, perfect, closing my eyes to imagine someone beside me, skin soft, firm muscles. Aching to love, to be loved.

The day that I first saw him as I left the cafe, the beach was empty, the footballers already sitting down, ordering drinks. He was leaning against the carob tree that grows at the edge of the beach and marks the place where that part of the beach starts, where the town people won't venture. Or where the men with families won't venture with their wives, mothers, children, but where they might come after dark when their women are safely taken home. Sometimes they come in small groups, to jeer. But

I've seen two or three come alone to look, and see if they too can catch a pretty boy.

That day he was leaning against the carob tree. He was different from the other young men who come to the beach, but I knew he belonged south of the carob tree. He didn't have his hair cut short, to reveal the shape of his head; an invitation to run your hands over it, to feel the shortness of the hair, to feel the curve of the skull. I have seen the boys on the beach and in the cafe joking and flirting, and so much innocent running of hands over shorn heads.

This boy, standing alone, had longer hair, a mass of dark curls. Sun glasses were pushed back on his head and at the front, two or three locks escaped. I wanted to twist his curls round my fingers, thread my fingers through his locks and then touch under his chin, and gently raise his face towards mine, bring my lips to touch his.

He was leaning against the tree, staring at the horizon. He must have become aware of me watching because he stood up and turned his head. He nodded, pulled his glasses over his eyes and set off into town. Maybe that was an invitation to follow, but I was in a cautious mood that day so I waited until he was almost out of sight before following the road into town.

I didn't see him again at the beach, but a few days later as I was going home after work, late at night, I met him.

'Can I walk with you?' he asked in formal Greek.

'Of course.' I looked over my shoulder.

'What's your name? I am Joseph. Joe.'

'Stephanos.'

'I am here for the summer. To work on the turtle project.' He looked at me to see if I understood.

'I guessed,' I said.

As we got into sight of the bay Joe said, 'Not there, let's go for a drink somewhere else,' and he turned up a sidestreet and into a taverna.

Inside it was dark; men sat on tall stools at the bar, watching a football match on satellite television. I looked round, no-one I recognised. A small room full of men. Not men like us. We drank small cups of coffee, glasses of local wine. I recognised the wine, it was from Nikos' father's vineyard.

I said that I knew about the project to protect the turtles. That it was a good thing for the island. I'd gone at night once and seen them, no bigger than a coin, scurry over the sand to the sea.

'And then they don't return for twenty years,' he said. 'The lost years. What do you suppose the turtles do all that time?'

Joe flirted, charmed me. But cautiously. He knew it was my place, my home.

'I come to help save the turtles. And see the beautiful island. And who knows what else I discover here.'

His head tilted, he fixed his eyes on me, parting his lips. So slightly. The football finished, or maybe it was just half-time. He leaned forwards.

'Let's go.'

* * *

In the morning I woke before him, lay still, my eyes shut against the sun, bright and hot already. This was the part where I always hoped I'd have courage. For a day together, a second night. To see if there could be more than lust, more than one sweet night of passion. But the bravado was gone, the effect of the drink and the night scents of bougainvillaea were spent. You see, for all my brave words, there is still fear.

Outside, the cockerel crowed. It didn't seem to keep to regular dawn hours. There was a change in Joe's breathing and the mattress shifted as he moved. He stroked my forehead and cheek, then lay a kiss on my chest, my solar plexus. I controlled my breathing, keeping it steady, my eyes closed.

He got up, made a drink, took a shower, sat on the bed beside me, bent over me, kissed my shoulder, made another drink. I kept still, my eyes tight shut, my breath controlled. Finally I heard him buckle his sandals, unlatch the door and slip out.

I waited a few moments and went downstairs, with apologies to the baker for oversleeping.

'No problem Stephanos.' He grinned. 'I heard you come in

last night. With a girl. Or perhaps a woman?'

I smiled, but avoided his eyes. He put his arm round my shoulder, pulled me to him.

'Heh! Good for you! There are lots of pretty girls here. You shouldn't be alone so much.'

The summer passed. After Joe, I spent my nights alone and eventually the winds started to bring in cooler air. I began packing my clothes, books, ready to go back to the village for the winter. At the restaurant our supplies were dwindling. We weren't offering such a range of meals.

It was the final weekend before the last charter plane left. Some places were already closed, the day after to-morrow and I'd be catching the bus up to the village. Couples who'd been here for the summer, enjoying each other in the sun were deciding what it meant, what to say, what to ask for, what to promise.

At the bar, it was after one before everyone was gone. I went outside to stack the chairs, sweep the floor. Two figures were still there, engrossed, making vows, remembering and planning, as lovers do. I looked away, banged the brush into table legs to make a noise, declare my presence. There was movement, chairs pushed as they stood up.

'Kalinkta.'

'Good night.'

Their voices spun down the street, muffled between the narrow closed-up shops. One voice, I recognised. And remembered. The caress of breath on my neck whispering to me. Joe, and a young man. Not Greek. Probably another volunteer with the turtles. They were taking a chance, indiscreet, but leaving to-morrow so who cared?

I locked up and walked out of town for about twenty or thirty minutes. A full moon was suspended over the sea. At the turtle beach a few bamboo sticks leaned over at odd angles, their yellow flags torn. It was a good stretch from the dunes where the nests were, across the sand to the sea. The lights from the bars along the coast road dazzled and confused the turtles, making them lose their way as they set out to scuttle over the beach. A dangerous crossing for a small turtle.

Going up the hillside the dark cypress needles marked the road the bus would take. In October there'd be the festival of Saint Georgios; he'd be there, the winegrower's son. No more avoiding, this time I'd talk. Find out about a different life. Too late with him. But not too late to be honest.

Down by the sea, the water ran up towards me, over my feet and then back down the sand. In the distance I imagined I saw a turtle, its shell glinting in the light from the moon.

Brothers Of The Hood

Len Evans

They could be four brothers, or mates, who'd hung
out as nippers in the sandpit of their local park,
sitting in a line, spitting to win twenty pence pieces.

Adults long gone, they'd inhabited the end house
on the estate with a forecourt to fit their passion
of four, maybe five cars max.

In summer, cool in cut offs and ripped sleeveless
tee shirts, they'd take shifts. Cutting and connecting,
oiling and waxing, overriding Girls Aloud on the radio,
if necessary, with their own strutting choreography,
moon walking between vehicles in full view of the bus stop.

After shifts, scrubbed up in pristine threads, they'd
come back for a night out; leaning against a polished hood
with a tinny, observing the others, smiling at their choice
of spanner, charmed by the multitasking of tyres, fan belt
and dip stick.

In winter, they'd erect a canopy in sub-zero temperatures,
wearing matching designer bobbles and stubble. On special
occasions they'd turn out in their full quartet, high fiving
pressing the starter motor, firing the ignition.

The thought of trying to get a girl on the back seat
never crossed their minds.

Dreaming Of Carpet Cleaner

Ruth Inglis

(In response to Dreaming of Rubber Gloves *by Jean Sprackland)*

You'd enter the supermarket
and listen to your heels
slap against the cool clean tiles.
You'd stride right past
the sweet and cake aisles.
You'd pick up the scent
of chlorine and bleach
infused with lemon and lavender,
you'd breathe in so deep
that the fumes would flood your brain
and guide your feet towards
the aisle labelled 'cleaning products'.
You'd leap across the threshold to explore
a gleaming gallery of glossy bottles
brandishing complicated labels
that you'd pretend to read and comprehend.
Then you'd see it and over you'd rush
to study the pink container, so bright it would
illuminate your cheeks as if you had blushed,
and once in your hand it would fit like a glove.

When you'd get back to your flat
you'd drop to the floor, scrubbing
out wine stains from the night before,
beads of sweat would surf across your frown.
You'd cast your mother's critical eye
over your new found domestic skills,
noticing a smudge on the wall, never seen before,
tomorrow you'd have to go back to the store.

Today I Changed A Baby

Glenn Carmichael

Today I changed a baby. I'd never done it before, see? I think I did quite well. Y'see, I slept with this woman, and she's a single mother, and she sleeps on a cheap futon, and it's close to the ground, and it's hard as hell down there – you can feel the floorboards. So anyway I didn't get too good a sleep, and once I was awake I just had to get up.

Now this woman is a late sleeper – I know that – and she'd said normally baby wakes her up, and she gives him a bottle and then he'll crash out again till half nine or so.

Well I woke up at seven, and baby's awake, but he seems happy enough, he's a very good baby, he just lies there and smiles a lot (sometimes I worry that he might have something wrong with him, y'know?). And so I'm looking at baby, and he's in a cot right next to the futon, right next to his sleeping mother, and I'm thinking, 'Poor baby probably got a dirty nappy.'

So I pick him up, take him into the living room, and I lay him on this plastic nappy changing mattress thing. And I get hold of a dry piece of cotton wool, thinking I'll take off his nappy and give his baby bot a wipe. And I take off his nappy and – wow – it's full of squidgy baby shit, and it smells and, oh my god I think I'm going to be sick. I mean I'm not always at my best first thing in the morning, and kind of normally I'd have to have a coffee before I do anything. A coffee, then a bowl of muesli, or something. But this is smelly kiddie crap for breakfast. And I don't know much about babies, and how best to remove nappies, or nothing like that, and all this kiddie crap comes as something of a very smelly surprise.

So I'm holding baby's legs in the air to stop all this kiddie cack going all over the place, and I'm holding the cacky nappy, and I've only got two hands, and it's all a bit much.

So anyway I manage to place this stinking nappy on the carpet without getting any crap on anything, but somehow I let go of one baby leg, and he sticks his heel on his bum and gets cacky kiddie crap all over the place. And I'm panicking a bit, and I think, 'Oh dear – I'll have to get him into the bathroom.'

So I picks him up and his head lolls backward, and I'm worrying about whiplash, and kiddie crap on my Levis, but somehow I get him into the bathroom and into the bath, and the enamel is cold this time of the morning, and nobody's put the immersion heater on, so I wash baby's bum and legs in cold water, worrying that he's going to be awful cold and start bawling, but this baby is as good as gold, and for all my apparent mishandling he seems quite content, in fact pleasantly spaced-out in a baby sort of way. He's watching the pattern the light makes through the thin, cotton, bathroom curtain.

So I wash all the shit away as best as I can, and I get baby dryish. And I manage to put a nappy on, assuming that the little pink and blue Teddies must go at the front on these disposable nappies, cos nobody's going to see them at the back. And I manage to fit it together quite good.

Then I go into the kitchen and get a bottle, which his mam had made up the night before, and I shove it in his mouth, and this he goes for in a big way. But he can't hold his own bottle for too long. So I'm kneeling on the floor, baby on the nappy changing plastic mattress, and I realise this could become very uncomfortable, kneeling here holding the bottle in baby's mouth. So I pick him up and I sit on a chair and cradle him in my arm, the way people do with babies, and I give him back his bottle and he's quite content and everything, just sucking away.

But after looking at him a bit, sort of studying the wonderfulness of a baby, I get a bit bored, and I'm so happy it's all going so well I think I'll sing him a little song. But I've never had a baby, and I'm thirty-six years old, and it's been a long time since I sang nursery rhymes. So I sing him an old Velvet Underground song about heroin. I'm singing it all soft and lovely, and I get to the part in the song saying, 'Cos it makes me feel like I'm a man, when I stick a spike into my vein,' and baby stops sucking and he gives me a beaming, beautiful, contented baby-bliss sort of a smile. And I realise I've done good with changing and feeding baby.

Eventually he finishes his bottle, and I put him back in his cot, all clean and fed and happy, and his mam carries on sleeping till 9.30, and I sat down and wrote this story.

Deadheading

Nina Boyd

She came in from the garden, where her mother
was chopping off the upturned faces of pansies,
took a pair of scissors and beheaded
a rag doll called Molly and a teddy called Sam.

Seeing no harm, she was sent away
to a school where the children were warned.
Matron's gift of an orphaned plush rabbit
was taken from her by the Head.

She carried her isolation forward, lived a long life alone,
only put to bed by someone who cared when dementia
left her speechless. She sat in rows
with listless women, flattened by drugs.

She was given a doll to cradle, told it was her baby.
Although she knew that there was not a jot
of life in it, she held it tight to her breast, crooning
as she wandered the corridors, looking for scissors.

The End Of The Pier

John Boyne

My sister, the writer Rosalie Stern, was talking about death. Her passing, she informed me, had taken place the night before in an accident over the Andes.

'I was in one of those old fashioned planes,' she explained. 'The ones they flew during the war where the pilot sits in a little... what's the word... pod at the front of the plane and the passenger, should there be one, sits separately, some distance behind. You see them in war films. There was a problem with the engine, I think. I remember flames.'

'And you died immediately?' I asked.

'Actually no,' she said, shaking her head. 'Mr Flynn did, of course. He was unrecognisable. But I was very badly injured. It was obvious that I shouldn't make any sudden movements.'

'And what happened then?'

'Well, I made a sudden movement,' she replied, smiling at me.

'And died.'

'Quite quickly. So what do you think, Roger? Can you explain it?'

'I'm afraid you haven't given me much to go on,' I said. 'I don't suppose you saw the funeral at all?'

'No.'

'Or any grief-stricken relatives?'

'Not a single one.'

'And Errol Flynn was definitely the pilot?'

'Most assuredly. Very dashing he was too.'

'But you've never been scared of flying in the past?'

'I wouldn't exactly say that I'm comfortable in a plane,' she said, giving my question some thought. 'However, I'm hardly what you'd call a nervous Nellie either.'

'The thing about dreams,' I said, 'Is that they're supposedly a subconscious representation of an unconscious desire. But they're just as likely to be an arbitrary series of thoughts put together to form a dramatic context.'

'Well it quite unsettled me,' she said with a slight shudder.

'I'm sure it did. No one likes to foresee their own death.'

'And such a brutal death, Roger,' she added, leaning forward and touching my arm, her fingers bone-chillingly skinny now, the skin wrapped around the ossified digits like tissue paper.

'But still,' I said, 'Just a dream. Nothing to worry about.'

'Well nevertheless, I've instructed William to cancel the Paris trip.'

'Rosalie, no!' I said, appalled, knowing how much she had been looking forward to it.

'No, no, I expressed that wrong,' she said, correcting herself. 'I've asked him to cancel the flights. We'll be going by ferry instead.'

'Worse still,' I muttered.

'We sail tomorrow evening,' she said. 'I hope it doesn't sink.'

'I hope so too.'

'You know, of course, that Aunt Helen went down on the Titanic?'

'Of course.'

'And Uncle Roger, for whom you were named, on the Lusitania?'

'Yes.'

'So it seems our family doesn't have much luck when it comes to sea voyages. We shall have to hope that I don't make it a triumvirate of Sterns buried at sea. If so, my dream will have had a bitter conclusion for without it, I never would have been on the ferry.'

'Life is a strange kettle of fish,' I said, for there was nothing else I could think of to say.

* * *

Later that afternoon, at home, I did two things that I hadn't done in a long time: I phoned my son, Philip, and I re-read my sister's first novel, The Emerald Princess.

'Your wife,' I said to Philip. 'How is she?'

'Very well,' he replied slowly, unsure why I was calling. We hadn't spoken in years. Mostly because he lives in Berlin while I refuse to leave London.

'I've always been fond of her,' I added. 'Witty woman, isn't she?'

'Extremely.'

'And handsome.'

'Very.'

'And that fellow she's married to now, what's his name?'

'Chancellor Eckhardt.'

'Yes, that's the one. He was here recently, you know. I saw him in the papers. Having dinner with the PM. Your wife wasn't there though. Thought that a bit odd.'

'She was in hospital,' explained Philip. 'Appendix.'

'Ah. That would explain it.'

'I believe the Chancellor considered staying with her but Greta wouldn't hear of it. Insisted he went.'

'She was always a pleasant-natured woman too.'

'Yes.'

'Why did you two call it a day?'

There was a pause at the other end of the line and for a moment I wasn't sure whether he'd heard me or not; I considered repeating the question but then his voice came down the line clear and unashamed, honest as the day is long.

'She didn't love me anymore,' he said. 'So it seemed like a bad idea to go on.'

'A sensible woman too,' I said. 'I thought of calling Downing Street to see if I couldn't get myself invited to the dinner but didn't bother in the end. Haven't been there in an age, not since Eden was making a shambles of things. I turned down an invite from Blair when he was in, on the grounds that I don't dine with homicidal maniacs if I can possibly avoid it. Although the truth is I quite liked him, actually – completely untrustworthy, of course, but I rather admire that in a chap – although she made my blood curdle.'

'Is everything alright, father?' asked Philip. 'Only I really should be getting back to work if there's nothing urgent going on.'

'Oh I don't want to keep you,' I said. 'I just thought I'd call, that's all. I had lunch with your aunt and she made inquiries after you.'

'How is she?'

'Very well. She doesn't have long left though. A strong wind could crumple her up.'

'Anything new on the way?'

'In September, apparently. A collection of stories.'

'I'll look out for it.'

'I'll make sure her publisher sends you a copy.'

'Lovely.'

'She's been having bad dreams lately,' I confided in him. 'Premonitions of her own death. That's what she wanted to talk to me about.'

'Old age, I expect,' said Philip. 'She must be nearly ninety.'

'She's eighty-eight,' I said sharply, defending her honour. 'Three years older than me. You young people don't think that age will creep up on you, but it does.'

'Father, I'm almost sixty,' said Philip. 'I have arthritis in my knee and my hearing is very poor. Sex would be a constant anxiety if I still had someone to have sex with. I'm hardly young.'

I grunted. I didn't want to discuss this. It's the strangest thing in the world but although I insist to people – accurately, as it turns out – that I am an old man, I never actually consider myself to be one. I don't remember how (or when) I got old. And I'm not in bad shape. But to think of Philip, almost sixty, arthritic, deaf and impotent, makes me want to take a pistol to my temples.

'You'll be home to visit soon?' I asked.

'Perhaps in July,' he said. 'There's an exhibition I'd like to attend.'

'Where will you stay?'

'The usual place.'

'We can have dinner.'

'I'll look forward to it. But nothing too rich. My doctor doesn't allow me to eat rich foods. Or meringues, strangely enough.'

'That's unfortunate. You were always partial to a meringue.'

'Yes.'

I got off the phone before he could lower my spirits any further and settled into an armchair with The Emerald Princess. Before starting to read, I looked at the author photograph on the back. My sister was only twenty-two when it was taken. The second world war was in full swing; she didn't look like she was even aware of the fact. Her expression could best be described as smug. Sort of a 'look at me with my metaphors and my similes and my big fancy hardcover, aren't I clever?' type of thing. She has, throughout her career, been plagued with unflattering descriptions of herself in the media as a cold, aristocratic novelist, a description I do not recognise for in truth, she's a warm-hearted, tender person, loyal to her friends and kind to her family. And a writer of quite extraordinary power.

Or so I thought.

When I first read The Emerald Princess I had just turned nineteen and thought it a work of genius. The story – quickly, I promise – concerned a young woman at the outbreak of the other war, the better war, living in London on quite good means. Through a series of misadventures she meets a young doctor who's working at a hospital for the returning wounded. They fall in love but he treats her shabbily on account of his being something of a cad. The war carries on, they continue their rutting among the wards and the broom cupboards and the beautiful shell-shocked boys, but when peace breaks out, he decides to leave London altogether. Heartbroken, our heroine does the decent thing. The title refers to a metaphorical story that the young man tells her at a crucial point in the yarn; I won't bore you with it. Anyway, my point being that at the age of nineteen, I thought the book a masterpiece and (I believed) this had nothing to do with the fact that its author was my sister, the writer Rosalie Stern.

However, I was wrong.

Re-reading it, I found it to be a tepid piece, full of ridiculous coincidence, arch dialogue and with rather too much of a tendency to ape the styles of Mrs Woolf and Miss Mansfield. I stayed with the book for most of the afternoon, growing more and more irritated by it, and when I reached the end, turning to the inside cover only to be confronted by Rosalie's smug smile, I really had to question what right she had to look so damned pompous. The book was nothing to be proud of. No wonder she never found a market in the Americas.

*　*　*

Some days later I found myself walking down Oxford Street in search of the business premises of Mr Albert Schneibel & Sons, a firm with which I have had sporadic dealings over the years. I first attended Mr Schneibel's store on the occasion of my Bar Mitzvah in 1931 when my late father brought me there to purchase a watch.

'Mr Stern!' cried Mr Schneibel as we entered his store all those years ago. 'You return to us!'

'I do, Mr Schneibel,' said my father. 'And how are you keeping?'

'Very well, thank you,' he replied in a lilting voice. 'A little of the hip, a little of the back, a little of the...' Here he tapped the side of his head and shrugged. 'But what can you do, eh? I should stand here and complain about it?'

'Sensible man,' said my father.

'And who is this gentleman?' asked Mr Schneibel, squinting his eyes to see me. 'This isn't Ludwig, surely? All grown up already?'

'Ludwig is far more grown up than this, Mr Schneibel,' said my late father referring to my late brother. 'This is Roger.'

'Roger?' asked Mr Schneibel. 'I haven't seen Roger since he was a baby.'

'Then you see him today, sir. Twelve years old, would you believe.'

Mr Schneibel shrugged his shoulders and, to my eyes at least, looked as if he had been insulted.

'What else can I do but believe?' he asked. 'Short of calling you a liar and claiming the child is not who you say he is.'

'Indeed,' said my father, smiling a little, a rare delight. 'Well Mr Schneibel, I'm happy to report that young Roger here has recently undertaken his Bar Mitzvah and to mark the occasion, I feel that a gift is in order. I would like, sir, to inspect your watches.'

Mr Schneibel stretched out an index finger and pointed it at me.

'The gift of a watch from a father to a son is a gift like no other. Do you understand that, young man?'

He spoke in a fierce tone, as if it was all he could do to restrain himself from boxing my ears. I nodded but remained silent; at this tender age my elders seemed to prefer it if I gave off the appearance of a mute when in company.

'Given the proper care, a watch purchased from Schneibel & Sons can be passed down for generations. Just make sure to wind it every night before bedtime and keep it away from water,' he added.

He disappeared into another room and returned with a tray filled with what to me looked like merchandise gathered from Aladdin's cave. The watches were perhaps the most beautiful items I had ever seen in my life, from that day to this, and that includes the voluptuous and much praised bosom of my late wife, Elspeth. My eyes opened wide as I stared at them, not daring to touch.

'Quite stunning,' said my father, picking one up and examining it carefully. 'Such craftsmanship!'

'Ah,' shrugged Mr Schneibel as if it was nothing when it was, quite clearly, something.

'What do you think, Roger? Do you approve?' asked my father and I nodded quickly.

'Yes, sir,' I replied.

'Which takes your fancy then? Be honest, now. Which one do you like the best?'

I hesitated and looked at them carefully. They each had their merits but there was one which stood out from the pack. It was a gold timepiece with a thin strip of silver between the rim and the glass. The numbers on the face were of a rich black embossed onto a startlingly white background. The fob was reassuringly large, the chain a badge of office. It was a watch which would endure. When I picked it up it felt heavy in my hands but I wanted to feel its weight in my waistcoat, pressed against my abdomen. I handed it to my father and he nodded.

'A fine choice,' he said quietly, admiring it.

'Very fine, you have a good eye,' said Mr Schneibel. 'A solid and sturdy watch. Masculine in its character but feminine in its beauty.'

'Then this is the one,' said my father, nodding his head and handing it to Mr Schneibel. 'You're happy, boy?'

Happy? Happy? Was the man mad? I am now eighty-five years of age and I can quite honestly state that the moment Mr Schneibel placed the watch in a box and presented it to me was the happiest moment of my life and that includes the moment Elspeth first allowed those voluptuous breasts to escape from their taut cotton captors into my outstretched welcoming palms.

'Thank you very much,' I said, unsteady words, unworthy ones, but to the point I suppose.

'You're most welcome,' said my father.

And that watch has seen me through seventy-three years from the morning after my Bar Mitzvah to the afternoon a few days ago when I finally had to admit that it had stopped working and wanted mending. And so there I was, wandering along Oxford Street in search of Schneibel & Sons but found myself unable to locate it.

I stopped a policeman by tapping his arm and would you believe it, the fellow told me off for assaulting him.

'Assaulting you?' I asked, unsure whether I had blacked out and taken my cane to him in a moment of madness, such as married politicians have on disreputable commons in the dead of night.

'You don't lay hands on an officer,' said the policeman who, on closer inspection, proved to be little more than a teenager with appalling skin and halitosis.

'I beg your pardon,' I said, unwilling to get into an argument, 'But are you familiar with the premises of Schneibel & Sons? They used to be here on Oxford Street – right here as I recall– but now there is this monstrosity.'

I was referring to something called a 'Pizza Hut'. Which is a restaurant. Of sorts. Apparently. Or so I'm told.

'Never 'eard of 'em, granddad,' said the fellow who I will not honour with the sturdy name of constable. 'What did they sell then?'

'Watches,' I said. 'Timepieces for the ages.'

He shook his head and scratched his chin. I noticed he hadn't shaved that morning.

'Sorry, granddad,' he repeated. 'Give Argos a go. They carry a decent range.'

A very unsatisfactory response, and one that left me walking back towards Tottenham Court Road an unhappy man.

Passing by a bookstore I took an urge for some fun and stepped inside to cheer myself up. I wanted my prejudices against the contemporary world confirmed once and for all. There were two young people standing behind the front counter, a boy and a girl in their early twenties, I would imagine. I hovered and listened to their conversation, which was trivial and not worth reporting.

'Rosalie Stern,' I said, approaching them.

'Pardon?' said the girl.

'I wondered where I might find Rosalie Stern.'

'Fiction,' said the boy.

'Round the corner there under S,' said the girl.

I must admit I felt disappointed. I expected them to say that no one of that name worked there.

'You're familiar with her work then?' I asked.

'Sure,' said the boy. 'Have you never read her?'

'No,' I lied.

'Start with The Man from Ethiopia,' said the girl. 'It's a very accessible introduction. See The End of the Pier as your final destination. Take a couple of months and enjoy the trip,' she added in a sing-song voice.

'You've read her then,' I asked, impressed beyond words.

'Of course,' they replied in unison.

'And who would you say are the contemporary writers who have been influenced by her the most?' I continued, genuinely interested now.

They considered this for a few moments and, after some debate, named three writers, a European gentleman, an American woman, and a Scottish playwright. Such diversity! A veritable United Nations of Literature!

'Well I must say, thank you for your time,' I said. 'It's been a pleasure talking to you.'

'No problem,' they said and turned back to their conversation about whatever entertainment they had attended the night before and I walked towards the door without buying anything. I felt a little embarrassed at myself, as if I had been trying to prove something that had turned out to be a falsehood. I left the bookshop feeling as a tart's client must after the event, when he has dressed and, murkily perspiring, is stepping back onto the street for the lust-drained trip home and the conscience-soothing relief of the bath.

Home again and this time to a letter from a Mr GF Willingham, estate agent, informing me that there were potential buyers interested in acquiring my home. This is not the first letter I have received from Mr GF Willingham; in fact it is the fourth in as many weeks. In each one he informs me that the area in which I live – Highgate – is a much valued one, that the road in which my home stands – Muswell Hill Road – is a much desired one, and that my own particular building – Southwood Hall – is a much admired one. It would not be difficult, Mr GF Willingham informs me, to find a buyer and he even claims to have parties interested already.

The first time I received the letter I simply crumpled it up and threw it away. The second time, I assumed there had been some mistake and discarded it again. On the third occasion I found myself growing irritable with his constant offers to evict me on to the street. But upon the arrival of that all too familiar envelope for a fourth time I confess that I saw red.

Firstly, contrary to what Mr GF Willingham may think, I do not own the whole of Southwood Hall. The house is divided over four floors, each one containing an apartment which is, compared to the modern dwellings I see on the television, extremely large. I have two bedrooms – my own and one for Philip, should he ever deign to stay here – two reception rooms, a kitchen, a pair of sprightly bathrooms, a vestibule, and an extraordinary view over Highgate Wood.

I have lived here since 1954, when I inherited it from my late

aunt and brought Elspeth here after our union. Together we lived in a state of unrelenting tension for most of our married life, punctuated by the birth, growth and escape of Philip. The floorboards contain the stories of my life. My possessions are scattered throughout and my library takes up every spare expanse of wall. The idea of leaving Southwood Hall compares with the notion of departing this world for the next, although bears little prospect of a similar reward. While many might consider my home to be cluttered, I would dispute the term.
I simply have a great deal of possessions, eighty-five years worth in fact, and cannot just discard things haphazardly like others do.

Mrs Bridge comes and does for me twice weekly and everything is kept ship-shape and Bristol fashion. Those who complain about the library taking over the living room would be astonished at the minimalist style and sparkling cleanliness of my bathroom. I simply know my priorities. I enjoy my books. I take pride in keeping clean. Is that so wrong? Not, of course, that I have many visitors but that's beside the point. Mrs Bridge and I share a pot of Darjeeling when we're both here but that's about it.

So Mr GF Willingham had rubbed me up the wrong way and I demanded satisfaction. I took my glasses off, the better to make out the small type at the top of his letter, and dialled his number on the telephone. A lady-receptionist answered.

'Good afternoon, Willingham & Co.'

'Good afternoon,' I replied. 'Mr GF Willingham, please.'

'Senior or Junior?'

'I beg your pardon?'

'Do you require Mr Willingham Senior or Junior.'

I sighed.

'I require the Mr Willingham who repeatedly sends me missives about purchasing my home,' I replied.

'Hold please.'

The receiver immediately began to emit sounds. It wasn't music, at least not as far as I understand the term. Finally the voice of a young man came on the line. He was laughing at something and did not seem to think it important to finish his conversation before beginning a new one.

'Twenty million quid he cost,' he cried out to an unknown listener, 'and he plays like a fucking fairy.'

'Hello?' I said, startled and appalled. 'Hello, is someone there?'

'Greg Willingham here,' said the young man. 'How can I help?'

'Mr Willingham, my name is Roger Stern,' I informed him, offering my address as back-up. 'I've received a number of letters from you regarding potential buyers for my home.'

'Great rental potential that, Mr Stern,' said GF Willingham. 'Very nice area too. Very des-res.'

'I'm aware of that. Which is why I live here.'

'Right. So have you found a new property yet or would you like us to help you with that too?'

'I think you misunderstand me, Mr Willingham,' I said. 'I don't wish to sell.'

'But you called about the letter.'

'Yes, to ask you to stop sending them.'

'Oh right,' he said, sounding a little deflated. 'Well, no harm done.'

'There is every harm done,' I replied. 'The cost to my back every time I lean down to pick up another of your unsolicited missives. The cost of this phone call. The cost of my time.'

'Listen, if you don't want to sell, you don't want to sell,' said GF Willingham.

'Can you take my index card out of your Rolodex then?' I pleaded. 'And stop sending me these letters. I grow weary of them.'

'Sure thing,' he said and for a moment I expected him to add a final insulting 'granddad', like the young police officer. 'But if you change your mind –'

'I will not be changing my mind,' I insisted. 'For one thing, should I leave Southwood Hall, where on earth would I go?'

He snorted down the phone, a delightful sound. 'Listen, with the money I could get you for there you could move into St James' Palace.'

'Oh no,' I said quickly. 'It's dreadfully draughty there. No, I couldn't do that.'

'We have some lovely new high-class apartments down

Clapham way.'

'Clapham?' I asked, laughing a little. 'Clapham?' I repeated, the ridiculous idea needing further expression. 'CLAPHAM?'

'It's very popular these days, sir.'

'Among a certain type of chap, perhaps,' I said. 'Of which I am not one.'

'Past all that, are you?' he asked with a laugh.

'Past it? I was never present at it!' I protested, shocked. 'I was married for over forty years! To Elspeth!'

'Well look, get in touch if you change your mind,' he said then, dismissing me as if the whole thing had been my idea in the first place and not his.

I wanted to express more indignation at Mr God Forsaken Willingham but the audacious pup had already hung up the phone. Needless to say, I discarded his letter immediately and swore that if another arrived I would consult Mr Hamish, my solicitor, about the matter.

Clapham! The very idea! Isn't that where chaps who enjoy the company of other chaps go?

* * *

I am having an early night tonight as I accompany my sister to Buckingham Palace in the morning where she is to be invested a Dame of the British Empire by HM. I confess that I'm quite looking forward to it. Mrs Bridge took my finest suit away to be dry-cleaned and it hangs in my wardrobe ready for the morning's excitement. I have bought new shoes for the occasion, which I worry was a bad idea for what if they start to hurt me en route? Not that there'll be an awful lot of walking, of course, for a driver is picking me up at nine to take me to my sister's house. From there, we go to the Savoy for breakfast and then onwards to greatness and posterity.

I've had the honour of attending the Palace twice before, once shortly after the war when a group of young civil servants were invited to dinner with the late King to celebrate the cessation of hostilities. We were a randomly selected group, there to represent the service as a whole, but I was a young man then and quite thrilled by it all. I managed a few words with the King after dinner when I inquired after the health of the Queen and he said she was very well, very well indeed. (She's not anymore, of course. She's dead. They all are. Everyone's dead now.)

The second time was during the 1980s when I accompanied my sister to a garden party to glorify various celebrated figures in the arts world, of which she was one. I was not in the best of twists at the time, my late wife having just achieved that glorified status a few weeks earlier and despite the constant anxiety of our household I found myself missing the old hag, and my sister brought me as her guest in order to 'get me out of myself' as she put it. It was a kind gesture but I found the afternoon intolerable, particularly as that awful Thatcher woman kept barking at me about what she'd like to do to the miners – murder them, castrate them, something along those lines, I imagine – and I even failed to recognise HM despite the fact that she was standing beside me, albeit without the crown. I believe there are those who thought I snubbed her, something I never would have done. HM knows her way around an engine as well as the best qualified mechanics and I admire her for that. It was the war training, you see; she had a good war, did HM.

However, if there are any hard feelings between the monarch and myself, they can be laid to rest tomorrow morning at the investiture, although I doubt she will remember me and Lord knows she has enough troubles of her own to contend with without worrying about the likes of me. Her children, for one thing, are cretins. Except Anne, of course. She's a handsome creature.

And so I go to sleep early tonight in the hope that I will be refreshed and alert for the morning. But as the light fades in my room I find myself troubled by my sister's dream of her death. It is true that we are all getting older; I am in my ninth decade of life and doubt that I shall live to see an eleventh. I can't complain. I have lived a reasonable existence and never been short of food, clothing or sustenance. But when I die there are certain things that I will miss, if I have a consciousness after the event. My library, for one. And Mrs Bridge, who's a dear. And it strikes me that for all people say about the world of today, it's not so bad really. For every policeman who abuses one on the street, there's a young bookseller able to hold a lively conversation in convivial surroundings about the work of an ancient scribbler.

Sleep gathers me within and it occurs to me that I am not afraid of dying, not in the slightest. I just don't want to, that's all. Life may hold a troubling set of irritations but nonetheless, I always look forward with a mixture of apprehension and delight to what the new day brings.

It keeps me young, you see. It keeps me alive.

The Shave

Glynis Charlton

She comes on a Monday (usually sneaks in)
takes things from a carrier,
carefully arranges them.

It's always the same (I've seen her),
the way she places stuff –
disposable razor, gel.

The old boy lies still (what else can he do?)
and lifts up his chin
as she spreads out the towel.

He's in the same gown (and yesterday's gravy)
but the towel is clean,
she can make sure of that.

The red bowl's gone missing (somebody's had it),
she finds it, half fills it
gets the water just right.

She squirt's the gel (it's cold on her palm)
and rubs it in round the old man's chin,
avoiding his mouth.

'Like this, remember?' she goes (like lipstick)
and he does as he's told,
a child being good.

He studies her face (two inches from his),
that little tip of tongue,
the way he concentrates.

There's trust in his eyes (not much choice really)
as razor drags stubble
tough as old boots.

Her fingers touch his cheek (ever so gently).
She can't look in his eyes –
the sharp blade would slip.

She wrings the flannel (not used since last week)
to wipe away foam
and pats his chin dry.

Folding the towel, she smiles (best she can)
and he smiles back, a good boy,
more stubble to come.

Da's Dublin 2008

Beda Higgins

She's scrubbed up well the dowdy old cow
slapped on lippy swishing rah-rah skirts up the Liffy.
Miss high and haughty with her historical ways,
Ah sure she's dancing with glee,
the bloody EEC detoxed her blocks,
spanking bright pavements and windows trailing
manicured geraniums, not dollops of manure.

Noble tourist buses boast every ten minutes
even the old asylum is a place of pride.
The lunatic driver sings sweet Molly Malone
as part of his St Patrick rehabilitation, while
fat Americans feel lumps in their throats
yanked out for their ancestral home.

Shops in matching shades, blink soft eyelid blinds,
batting welcome to our humble abode. Pretty bows
next to cafes with designer ham, cabbage and mash.
Temple Street no longer a brawling tart in the gutter
flashing her knickers and puking up the day,
but a slip of a girl sipping water, not jarred poteen.

And she's so clever with her book of Kells,
and everyone's churning out Celtic culture,
the brains of the brawn is awesome.
My Da would be proud to dance with Dublin
her streets jigging him a merry reel,
but he'd never forgive her, no fecking smoking?
Making yesterday's city a sweeter streel.

26,298

Mick Haining

He waited until the man passed him, then picked up the empty beer can and put it in the plastic bag with the others. It irritated him mildly that, after all these years, he still felt faintly embarrassed about it. 'Four,' he counted inwardly. It wasn't many for the walk and again he felt caught between being glad and dissatisfied that there were so few. He straightened and looked at the swollen river. In over thirty years of living there, he had never seen it so high – another foot and it would be lapping the top of the embankment. The sun was shining now but that, too, was a cause of mixed feelings. Yes, it was nice that the rain had finally stopped but no, the snow melting more rapidly on the hills would not be good news. He sighed. 'We're never satisfied,' he thought as he continued his walk.

At home, he took out his notebook and added four onto the total. Mahatma jumped onto the table and stepped onto the notebook, pushing his head against John's chin.

'I hope you can swim,' said John.

His son, Phil, rang shortly afterwards.

'I'll come down straight after work and help you shift a few things upstairs,' he said.

'No need,' said John. 'I'm on with it.'

'Dad!' said Phil. 'You're 72, not 27. Don't shift anything heavy.'

'I'll have to put the phone down, son,' said John, 'I've got the sofa in my other hand and I can't hold both.'

'Don't you ever take anything seriously?' said Phil. 'Just make sure you get your photos and your diaries up there. Insurance will pay for a new sofa.'

When John replaced the receiver, he smiled. He did not feel 'old', but he knew he felt a lot more aches than he had at 27. Mahatma was curled in front of the fire.

'You just take it easy,' said John, 'I'll call you if I need you.' Mahatma's ears twitched.

The radio told him that the flood warning for the area was now severe. John moved his diaries upstairs first and then his scrapbooks. He was quite breathless when he began to stack the boxes of photos. They were, of course, too tempting. Little surges of affection rose in him as, in moving the disordered collection from the chest to bags and boxes, he caught sight of earlier days – Lizzie holding little Phil above the waves, Phil in his Postman Pat apron, Lizzie asleep on the steam train journey, Lizzie, Lizzie, Lizzie... occasionally, he sighed, too. The police siren burst into his nostalgia. A loudspeaker was calling on residents to evacuate the area. He went to the door and opened it as a policeman hurried up the path. John reassured him that his son was on his way and the young policeman almost ran off. If Phil hadn't shut his school by now, though, then it might actually be an hour or so before he arrived. Still, thought John, the police have bigger fish to fry.

'Fish,' he echoed to Mahatma, picking up a couple of boxes of photographs.

'You might be meeting a few soon.' Mahatma suddenly lifted his head and listened. He rose and ran quickly to one side of the room, then the other.

'I've made worse jokes,' said John, but Mahatma's behaviour made him feel a little uneasy.

He went again to the front door and looked out. He stared. He could see water moving along the road. It wasn't in a hurry, but it was steady. John moved up the stairs as quickly as he could with the photographs. He hurried down for more and Mahatma ran in front of him, almost tripping him. He briefly recalled how silly he'd felt calling 'Mahatma' into the garden on the nights when Mahatma had gone 'clubbing', as Lizzie used to call it. As he passed the front door with the last photographs, he glanced and saw water easing its way slowly up the front path.

Upstairs, breathing hard, he dropped the photographs hastily onto the bed and saw Mahatma scratching to get into the wardrobe. He was forming a joke about Noah's Ark when startling pain struck inside his chest. He fell against the bed, among his memories, and could only think, ridiculously, that he was 47 cans short.

In hospital, he explained it all to Phil.

'A can for every day I've been alive,' he said. 'I wrote enough letters complaining and then, one day, I thought, why don't I just pick them up, you know, a few at a time... well, I was passing them every day and they weren't going anywhere. If everybody looked after their own patch, there wouldn't be such a problem.'

'But over 26,000!' said Phil. 'Surely there couldn't have been over 26,000 dropped from here to town?'

'I took the odd detour,' said John. 'You'd be surprised. Twelve years, mind you. But I still have a few to go.'

'It might be a few more than you think,' said Phil. 'Your recycling boxes went for a cruise, too. And you can't go humping heavy weights around now – you heard what the doctor said about your heart.'

'I'm going to fit a little cart to Mahatma,' said John. 'He empties enough cans of his own.'

After Phil alerted them, the local paper ran a feature on John. The photographers brought a couple of empty cans into the hospital and John felt embarrassed posing with them. The following week, there were several supportive letters, but, after that, John was relieved to find no references. By then, he had been established in Phil's house for several days. The long wait for his own home to dry and be renovated had begun.

It was late summer before Phil finally drove him back. They walked together up John's front path. Mahatma stopped to sniff and then disappeared around the side of the house.

'I remember the day I carried you up here for the first time,' said John. 'You reached out and touched the door before me and said 'House!'.

'We do need to talk about you living here on your own, Dad,' said Phil.

John shook his head as he unlocked the front door.

'I don't want to be where your mum wasn't,' he said.

The street held a party to celebrate when everybody had returned. It was a chance to exchange stories of alarm, destruction, rescue and insurance. Neighbours who rarely spoke chatted as if to long-lost friends. Laughter and music carried on beyond the fading of the light, and John listened, smiling, from his bed. He had enjoyed the day but ten o'clock was his limit.

In the morning, he rose and opened the curtains onto Sunday sunshine. He looked down at the street where the debris from the party had partially been cleared. Something seemed odd about it. As he stared, he realised that most things had been cleared – the paper plates, streamers, bits of food had all been collected in bin bags. He could see cardboard boxes full of empty bottles. The only things not to have been collected were the empty cans.

After a late breakfast, he went to the front door and then to the gate. The full bin bags and the bottles had been taken away, but the cans lay where they had been left. There were a couple of folded bin bags by his gate. He stood for a few moments, puzzled. Mahatma came to have a look and stood with his tail twitching.

'What do you think?' said John. 'Heads I pick them up.' He tossed an imaginary coin in the air. 'Damn,' he said. 'I knew it would be heads.'

He picked up a bin bag and put the first can into it. 'One,' he said to himself and moved to the next. After he had picked up about a dozen, he heard a front door open. He gritted his teeth and continued. 'Don't look up,' he said to himself. Then the clapping began. He stopped and looked up. All along the street, the neighbours were at their doors and they were looking at him, smiling and applauding. The applause was loud and sustained. He began to smile himself and then to laugh.

'You buggers!' he shouted. 'You daft buggers!' He continued his collection.

'It was hard work emptying them for you!' called James, 'but somebody had to do it!'

'Let us know if you're short!' shouted Tommy. 'We'll see what we can do!'

'We might need another party!' replied John.

He carried on along the street, laughing, picking up and counting empty cans.

I Love

Martin Wickham

Her wonky eye and crooked tooth.
The smell of her breath after a packet
of cheese and onion crisps,
it makes my nostrils bleed with undying devotion.

The long hairs she leaves in the bath
woven like a spider web in the plug hole.

Her knickers and socks that decorate our floors and sofas,
feng-shui-ing our lounge.

Her apologetic farts and burps,
knuckle cracks and smelly feet.

The way she can crawl under my skin
with a single shrug or raised eyebrow.

Her mocking grin when my tongue tangles a sentence
and her cackle when she corrects me.

Then sometimes she smiles,
and laughs,
and fits into my arms with her head resting on my chest
a recess big enough for only her to fill.

Love Poem No 32

Justine Warden

Do you remember Julie London in the 50s?
You remember that look she had?
It said, I am a singer of smoky jazz but I know 32 ways
to convince yourself your heart is sturdy

Do you remember Jane Fonda in the 60s?
You remember that look she had?
It said, I am a movie star but I know 32 ways to kill you
with a single sheet of paper

Do you remember Marvin Gaye in the 70s?
You remember that look he had?
It said, I am a sex god but I know 32 ways to hide quietly
until they all go away

Do you remember Margaret Thatcher in the 80s?
You remember that look she had?
It said, I am the Prime Minister of a Democratic country
but I know 32 ways to take you down, son

Do you remember you, three years ago?
You remember that look you had?
It said, at last.
But I know 32 ways to have my cake and eat it.

Sonnet 155

Anna-Marie Vickerstaff

Shall I compare thee to a summer's day?
Then wilst thou answer my fucking text?
I'm sorry you don't get sonnets from me,
but who d'you think you are? Petrarch's ex?

Oh let my books then be my eloquence
Wyatt and Surrey ain't got shit on me!
I'll be a hound, chase a deer past the fence,
pick a conceit, I'll rewrite it for thee.

Call you the marigold in the sun's eye,
but it seems you, my son, have hayfever.
Carve my love, you spit in my face and cry
of my uniambic pentameter.

Fuck it! Because no matter how I strive,
you're still waiting, for Shakespeare's 155.

Between Floors

Cath Humphris

I finally found God in an attic flat near the centre of Gloucester. A dim and dingy room, its only furniture was an enormous table covered with scientific apparatus. Not the kind of surroundings one connected with a celestial being, and I told her so. She looked as dingy as the room.

'Washing my hair isn't a priority,' God said, running grimy fingers through the limp strands. 'If I'd known I was about to be interviewed for the... Scientist Times... so sorry to disappoint.'

I called her attention to several well established art masters of the renaissance period as support for my opinion.

To be fair, it was obvious that I had interrupted at a critical moment. While she attended to me the chemicals in the flask she was heating became violently irritated and spontaneously combusted. There was an almighty explosion.

'Michelangelo,' she shouted. 'What would he know?'

A man below banged on his ceiling, threatening to call the bomb squad and the police.

God laughed, not something I expected from an august deity. But then, I had not expected to find her in the attic of a bed and breakfast hostel in the centre of Gloucester.

* * *

Always I had been too late. That last morning in Cartagena I must have passed her on the stairs to the apartment.

'Si, God was here. She just go,' the neighbour told me. 'Maybe five minutes.'

But when I ran back down there was no sign. It was mid-day; the street was already subsiding for siesta.

The neighbour was sure she would be back. He showed me the wardrobe of clothes she had left, a rainbow of bright drapery in clinging designs. They were sleeveless, with artful gathers and slits: hot urban fashions. When I held one of them against me it was surprisingly small and pristine, I wondered if any had been worn.

'Ah,' sighed the little man as he took back the flimsy fabric and placed it on the rail. There were no personal items, not even perishables left in the ice box. I opened empty drawers in the moments before he herded me out and locked the door. He refused my money but invited me to eat with him.

The heat was thick, even in that white room with its shutters filtering the sun. I longed for the foggy chill of a Bristol winter.

I had been following rumours across the continents for six months. Sometimes I was days late, others an hour. The trail had led me to the most dreamed of corners of the world: limpid tree lined rivers in Africa; the crumbling edges of Antarctica and across the frontiers of Asia. I saw more beauty and destruction than I could bear but there was never time for more than a glancing attention. Always I arrived just too late.

With polite gallantry my elderly host drew out a chair and seated me at the table. He fetched spiced fish, salad and rice and poured iced coffee from a glistening jug into stem glasses.

When I complemented him on the meal he smiled and nodded.

'Almuerzo,' he said. His English deteriorated to the level of my Spanish as the meal progressed and I was learning nothing.

'Gracias' I said, toasting him.

He mistook my gesture and reached across to refill my glass, laughing when I tried to refuse. The drink was refreshing but potent, as was his expression. I did not need a translator. He rested his elbow on the table and leaned forward. The intimacy of his attention took my breath away. I gazed into youthfully intent blue eyes and was unable to stop myself drifting towards him.

That night I phoned my editor.

'There's no pattern,' I told him. 'I'm not even sure it's her.'

'What do you mean?'

'This isn't the same woman.'

'You've seen her?'

'These clothes are smaller, younger than the ones left in Tokyo.'

I heard his chair creak and pictured him swivelling round to the view across office blocks and the river. I longed for that wall of tinted glass and an invisible atmosphere.

'This was just a new-ager spending her lottery win or her alimony,' I said.

'Don't lose sight, you're nearly there. I know it.'

'Send someone else.'

'Go back to the neighbours, find out what she was wearing when she left.'

'I've booked a ticket home.'

* * *

God was wearing a blue nylon overall. She looked as if she fried chips for a living and the weight of her movements suggested that she ate them, regularly. There was no way to record the interview. My phone had been in my pocket when I left home, but must have got left at the office in the rush to meet my informant.

'The Sistine chapel?' God snorted and began counting off the fingers of her left hand, 'Cerulean blue, gleaming white hair and lots of firm flesh tangled up in reams of sheeting.' She shook her head. 'You think it's that easy?' She lifted up the sooty flask, which had somehow survived the blast.

'Ignore him,' she said, when I suggested we apologise to the man below. 'He's been following me about for months. He's always complaining and wasting police time.'

Remembering the stairs I thought it possible God's neighbour had a point. The stink in the hall and stairway had increased in strength and density as I made my way up to God's room. In fact, for the last few yards I had stumbled through thick yellow fog.

I made a few suggestions along the lines of neighbourly behaviour. Not working after 11pm seemed a good start.

'And you could open the window while you're heating up those mixtures, this one smells worse than kippers.'

God put her head up and sniffed.

'Kippers? I would have said roses myself, and strawberries. Then there are new potatoes, violets, ripe plums, crushed grass, basil, thyme and rosemary... rather pleasant I like to think.' She inhaled deeply again and sighed. 'Yes. It's getting there.'

'You wha...?' I faltered. My mind fumbled, because as she spoke, I could indeed detect each of those things and a thousand more. The shabby room seemed filled with fresher, sweeter air than I had ever inhaled before.

'Wow, beautiful,' I said. 'Amazing. What are you going to call it?'

'Flora.'

I thought it somewhat unoriginal, but I smiled and offered congratulations. She wasn't listening. She was sifting through a pile of junk on the far side of the table, muttering to herself. 'Rubber... no... no good. Piece of cork, that might do... might contaminate it though.'

Fascinated, I listened in to that process of elimination. This was the kind of insight my editor wanted, the workings of a sublime mind.

'Ah, that's the one, must let it breathe.' She had picked something up and turned away before I had chance to identify it. Deftly she inserted the blob into the open end of the blackened flask before carrying it across to the far corner of the room, where she placed it in a rack on a high shelf.

I could just make out the shapes of two other tubes there. I longed to ask about them, but God was busy at the table clearing away bottles and phials. She treated them with an alarming lack of care, more or less scooping them into a cardboard wine carton. I winced as the glass clinked, and wondered aloud that she was not more careful with her chemicals. For the first time I saw her display genuine amusement.

'Me, have an accident?' The room seemed to shake with her laughter as she reeled around it holding onto her belly and roaring till tears flowed down her cheeks. 'Oh, oh ho ho. I might poison... ha ha ha. Me... destroy?'

I told her I was not joking, but that made her laugh all the more. I was beginning to get irritated, and was not surprised when the banging from below started again. The poor man was probably shaken from his bed. I had to grab hold of the door handle in order to stay upright. Everything else in the room was bouncing about as if we were in an earthquake.

Just then the Southgate chimes began to ring. God sobered up instantly. She careered over to the window and after rubbing the grimy pane with her sleeve peered down through the glass.

'Midnight,' she cried, and turned. Her voice was cold and angry. 'You,' she raised her right hand and I seemed to feel her pointed index finger hard in the centre of my chest. 'You've put me off schedule. I should have started stage four by now. All this chatter is getting in my way, you'll have to go.'

My knees gave way. I tried to stammer out an apology, a plea for mercy, but she was not listening. When I looked up she was already busy at the table, clipping together a complicated formation of tubes and pipes.

I rose shakily and fumbled with the handle of the door.

'You can leave that.' God said.

She was looking at my knees. There was a thick layer of grey dust on my jeans. When I went to rub at it she handed me one of those plastic fluff removers that are really just another way of selling sticky tape.

'Didn't your mother teach you anything about personal hygiene?' she said.

Astounded, I removed the offending dust and laid the gadget on a corner of the table. Almost absentmindedly God picked it up and as I turned at the door she pulled a heavy cardboard box out from under the table. She lifted up a huge alembic, and balancing it against her hip, began to pick pinches of fluff from the tape and drop them into the sphere.

Although nowhere near the Bunsen burner, the sphere seemed to be going through a chemical reaction. A dense dark cloud formed and tiny reflective particles appeared. I was tempted to question her about processes and ingredients, but without turning God yelled for me to get on out and close the twice damned door.

The air in the hall had cleared slightly. I made my way to the stairs and became aware of that fungal odour I had noticed before. The light bulb on the landing had failed. The only illumination came from the narrow gap beneath God's door.

Oddly, although I had found the interior of her room dim, the light now escaping seemed amazingly bright. When I turned off those stairs onto the lower landing I stepped into complete darkness. I had to grope my way along to the second staircase, dreading to think what the spongy substance beneath my feet might be. I decided to throw my shoes away as soon as I got home.

A man was waiting at the bottom of the stairs. He was dressed for a dinner party. I had the impression that he had been that way for a long time, possibly years, judging by the faded colour of his cumber band.

He reminded me of the costume-dolls that my old aunt displays in her glass cabinet. Even in the soft light glowing from his partially open door his clothes had a dusty, felted look to them. As he moved, the buttons of his waistcoat gaped open and I caught glimpses of an under-garment in a much richer shade of red.

When I attempted to sidle past he grabbed my arm and leaning forward said, in a pilchard scented gust of breath,

'I don't care who she is, she's out Saturday, and him too. Good riddance to the pair of them.'

Before I could reply he shuffled back inside. I caught a glimpse of the interior, faded grandeur it looked like. There was a tall candelabra dripping wax onto a worn oriental carpet and cats. More cats than I could count came slinking towards him. They rubbed against his legs and stretched up his body as if to hug him.

'There's no leeway. A week, that's all she paid for,' he shouted. Then he slammed his door, leaving me to grope for the way out in darkness.

As I stepped onto the street it struck me that he and his tenants were ideally suited, and it could only be a matter of time before someone reported all three of them to social services.

Story Without Meaning

John Brown

'Well, I can see you're not a dick.' Said God. I was sitting in the largest of the three dressing rooms drinking a tin of Tennent's with God. He was smartly dressed, in a navy blue suit, a pair of shiny Oxfords and a crisp white open necked shirt. His hair was medium length and light brown. He was clean shaven. His eyes were a pale blue-grey. He was medium height with a slightly stooped gait. He looked to be in his mid-fifties but obviously that was an illusion.

He wasn't what I expected exactly. I'd told myself for months, to keep an open mind. He wasn't going to fit any stereotype. But for some reason, I'd had this image of Charlton Heston when he played Moses in The Ten Commandments. Why Moses? Well, I suppose he looked biblical. Like the god that Michelangelo painted. In fact, the more I considered it, the more the depictions of God I had seen all looked pretty much the same: stately, noble, long grey hair, beard, nice tan, white smock or bare chested and rippling with elderly muscle – like a stockier Iggy Pop. But of course these were western depictions. Quite different from Krishna or Buddha or Apocatequil.

Van Eyck's God was a bit more pimped up with lots of gold and rubies. Del Castagno, Quellin, Michelangelo – they all showed him looking a bit cross. But here he was sitting opposite me, looking quite relaxed, a bit bored if anything.

He reached into his inside suit pocket and pulled out a packet of Benson and Hedges.

'Is it alright to smoke in here?'

He looked around the room.

'Er, no, sorry, it's not.' I pointed to the smoke alarm. I felt a bit foolish telling God not to smoke.

He tapped me on the shoulder.

'I hear what you're saying cocker,' he said and took out a cigarette anyway. He put it in his mouth and lit it with a cheap disposable lighter. So what if the alarm went off, what was front of house going to do? They couldn't exactly throw God out of the building could they?

'So what we gonna talk about?' He said.

'Well, I thought we could start with Richard Dawkins.'

'Who?'

'He's a scientist, written a lot about you not existing.'

'Oh right.'

He shrugged as though the subject was pointless, which I suppose now it was.

'I've prepared some questions,' I said, 'but I'd rather it was more like a conversation. I thought we could see how it goes.'

'Fine by me.' He said, and flicked his ash on the floor. I looked up at the alarm, it hadn't gone off. Sign of divine intervention? He took a long drink from his tin.

'Listen,' he said, 'Come and get me at quarter past seven. We'll have a glass of that champagne.'

Then he put the tin down and shooed me off. But it didn't feel discourteous. Just like he was tired and had what he needed. He'd been appraising me, that was all, seeing who I was.

I went out to the front and peeked at the crowd from a gap in the door. The event had sold out almost immediately, months ago now, when I first advertised it. I could have got a bigger venue, charged more for the tickets, but it was daft to think about that now. I'd chosen this venue because I liked the acoustics and because it was nice and light and airy. I wanted the audience to ask questions and it was important that the space wasn't too intimidating. I'd thought about using the cathedral but the acoustics were a bit echoey. I'd worried that God wouldn't really come across very well, assuming that his voice would be big and boomy. But in actual fact it was, if anything, a bit nasally.

The BBC film crew were already in the theatre. I'd sorted out two boxes for their cameras either side of the stage. Other media companies had offered more money, but I thought it was better that it was the BBC – seemed more appropriate for the occasion. Sky just didn't seem pious enough, nor did Fox.

When I was little and it was time for bed my mum used to tell me a story. It was always me who would get her to tell it.

'Tell me about the sexton.' I'd say.

'You know what a sexton is don't you?' She'd say, and I'd tell her a sexton was someone whose job it was to tend to the graves. She knew that I knew the answer, and I knew that she knew that I knew that answer. It didn't matter. It was a ritual. And then she'd tell the story.

'Once upon a time there was a sexton and one day he was tending a grave when a cat walked up to him on its two hind legs. He was wearing big black boots and a hat and he said to the sexton, "Tell Tom Tiddledum that Tim Toddledum is dead." Now the sexton was so taken aback to meet a talking cat that he said, "Pardon" even though he'd heard everything the cat had said. The cat looked irritated but then said again, "Tell Tom Tiddledum that Tim Toddledum is dead." And with that he walked off leaving the sexton scratching his head...

That night the sexton came home from work and was greeted by his wife. He sat at the table and she served him his evening meal.

"So, how was your day?" She said.

"Well, to be honest, a bit strange."

"Oh really, why's that?" She said.

"Well, I was out in the graveyard tending to a grave when this cat walked up on its two hind legs. It was wearing big black boots and a hat and said, tell Tom Tiddledum that Tim Toddledum is dead."

His wife raised her eyebrows and asked the sexton to repeat what he had said, even though she heard him quite correctly the first time.

"Tell Tom Tiddledum that Tim Toddledum is dead." And as he said this a little louder than the first time, their old cat Tom, who had been sleeping by the hearth, leapt up and said,

"Hooray, I'm king of the cats!" and ran off.

Old Tom was never seen again.'

'What does it mean?' I'd always ask my mum, but she would just smile at me, kiss me on top of my head and say good night. I was sitting in the smallest dressing room on my own looking over my list of questions. They all seemed rather pointless, he doesn't even know who Dawkins is, so that's the first set of questions out of the equation. The more I looked at the list the more I could feel my heart pound and my mouth go dry. I was very dreadfully nervous. Part of me just wanted to ask him, but what does it all mean God? But it was too naive a question. Too open, unfocussed. How was he supposed to answer that?

I looked at my watch, not long now. The fear had been building since I'd first sent out the press releases. It came in waves. Some days it was unbearable and I'd think about calling the whole thing off, but then a voice would say, don't be stupid, this is going to be the most important moment of your life. I'd been having nightmares, waking up screaming, lying in my own sweat. My wife thought it was a stupid idea, but I knew in the end, that I'd have to do it and that it would be done.

I'd asked other people at first. I tried David Attenborough, Germaine Greer and Morgan Freeman. I wrote to Parkinson and Richard Dimbleby. I thought Will Self might be interested and I contacted him through his agent. Maya Angelou, Bill Clinton, Gore Vidal, Salman Rushdie, Joanna Lumley. They all turned me down. It was too risky. There was too much at stake. Joanna Lumley had wished me luck in her email, she herself was tied up. Then that voice again, you can do it, don't worry about it. You'll be fine. But I didn't feel fine now. I finished off the tin of Tennent's. I need another, I thought and I walked down to the green room. I went over to the fridge and pulled out another tin. I prised it open and took a gulp.

Come on, this is it. You can do it, you're King of the Cats. I tried to recall the lyrics to that Eminem song: his palms are sweaty, knees weak, arms heavy... Yep, that just about described it. I tried to take Eminem's advice, to capture the moment and lose yourself in it. I took another gulp. God's rider had surprised me, 48 tins of Tennent's, two packets of Benson and Hedges and a bottle of champagne. He could knock back the ale, no question about that. No one was going to drink God under the table.

But this was all voodoo. He was just trying to psyche me out. What he wanted from me was to step up to the stage and take him on as an equal adversary. Well, fuck it, I was going to do it. I drank another mouthful of beer then reached for the chilled bottle of champagne. I took two glass flutes and walked towards God's dressing room.

'Good evening ladies and gentlemen and welcome to this event, which as you know is God in conversation in front of a live audience. Now, I know what a lot of you are thinking, has he turned up? Right?'

This got a bit of a laugh and made me relax a little.

'Well he has, so don't worry, he's waiting in the wings now and I'll get him out on stage in a minute. Before I do, I'd just like to say a few things. When I invited God to come and talk to me at this event, it was really just a pipedream. I'd talked about it a lot with friends and colleagues and they'd all laughed or said that I was mad. Then one day, I thought, what the hell, why not? What's the worst that can happen? So I plucked up all the courage I could muster and wrote to him. When I finished the letter, I wasn't sure what to put on the envelope, but in the end just settled for 'God'. I'd had quite a bit to drink, I don't mind admitting, when I posted it later that night. Then I forgot about it. It was such a daft idea. So imagine my delight and surprise a few weeks later when I received a reply.'

I could feel the crowd fidget, better get on with it.

'But look, you've not come here to listen to my ramblings, we all know why we are here. He doesn't need any introduction so let's get him on stage now. Please, put your hands together to welcome on stage... God.'

* * *

Five minutes in to the conversation and things were already starting to fall apart.

'Have you ever met the devil?' I asked.

'Is that the best you can do?' He looked genuinely disappointed at the level of our conversation and I felt dismayed. I'd let him down.

'What about Iraq?'

'What about it?'

'Why don't you intervene?'

He stared at me for a long time. I got an electric jolt right through my body. I felt my internal temperature drop two degrees.

'Now don't get clever sunshine.' He said at last.

Shit. This is going terrible. Even worse than I thought it was going to go.

I could feel my palms getting all clammy. I kept wiping them on my trousers. I could hardly swallow my throat was so dry. I asked him a few more questions but all I got back was a yes, a no, or a don't know. The crowd were getting restless, agitated. Someone three rows back shouted, 'this is boring.' Someone else in the upper circle shouted, 'I paid fifty quid for this?' I tried to keep a lid on it. I changed the subject.

What had he been doing all these years?

'None of your fucking business,' he said.

That got a laugh. I was playing stooge now but it wasn't working. I had run out of things to say, or rather I had lost confidence to ask him anything. Someone else shouted,

'My mum's just died of cancer and it's your fault.' Then someone threw a bottle and it just missed my head. I stood up, angry now.

'Who threw that?'

But it was too dark to make anything out in the audience.

'What about the Holocaust?'

'What about Rwanda?'

Another bottle. Then God stood up.

'I think that's it,' he said. And without another word he wandered off.

Backstage I was close to tears. I could hear the crowd shouting. Twenty minutes, that's all I'd managed. And not one answer worth the price of the ticket. Nothing. I couldn't blame them. I had failed completely. What was I thinking about? No wonder Joanna Lumley had wished me luck. I went to the green room and reached into the fridge for a tin of Tennent's. There were only a dozen or so left. I drank the lager in huge gulps. Then I heard the dressing room door go. Next the door of the green room opened and in walked God. He nodded acknowledgement then walked over to the fridge. He took out a carrier bag from his suit pocket and filled it up with the remaining tins.

'Look God, I know I made a balls of that, but can I ask you one last thing?'

'Go ahead.' He closed the fridge door and walked towards the back door exit.

'It's just something... I know it's a... well, what I was going to ask is, what does it... what does it all mean?'

He'd opened the back door exit and was standing at the threshold. He beckoned me over. As I got close he looked at me and smiled to himself, then he shook his head.

'You've got a fucking cheek haven't you..? Listen,' he said, 'you did alright.'

He put the bag of beer down. Then he took my head in his hands and kissed me on my forehead.

'Relax, don't worry about it son,' he said. 'Pretty soon it will all be over and then it won't mean anything, again.'

He picked up the bag and walked along the corridor leading to the fire exit. I followed him. I wanted to ask him something else. The door closed automatically behind me and we were both in darkness briefly, until God reached the fire escape and pushed the bar which opened the door. For a moment he was lit up in a rectangle of white light, his light brown hair a halo of gold, then he closed the door behind him, leaving me in a long dark corridor with a closed door at either end.

Teaching Beginners Poetry

Fiona Durance

I tell them to suck their tongues –
feel the plump non-taste of it, its muscularity
and force. Then run the tip around the inside
of the lips, feel the contrast, the smoothness.
And then the teeth, the mouth's sturdy monuments –
explore each one, its every dimple and ripple,
the line where it sinks beneath the gum, the place
where feeling starts. Then the alveolar ridge –
glide up that upside-down slide to the mouth's roof
and fall back to the limp, curtain-like layers. The sleek,
almost featureless cheeks. And there, inside the corral
of the lower teeth, the soft, lumpy undertongue, the thin,
restraining membrane. I ask them to picture it all –
the agile flesh, the wet red skin, the purple of veins.
The grey, white or yellow of teeth, with their caves of decay
or their hoards of silver and gold. The remnants of dinner,
trapped meat fibre or corn-skin sliver, the amount and type
of saliva. Track it all. Discover it like a new territory,
an adventure holiday. Know it from the inside. Like a lover.
Like being born. Like dying. Know it for the first time. Like living,
really living. Feel it, taste it, notice it all. The tongue's fast gymnastics
as it moulds and tips words. The shape of the words
still untold.

This Is Disaster Poetry

Andrea Tang

The swarm smokes its carbon-tine cigs,
pushes burning stumps into ice glasses at the Arctic Club.
The vodka level rises and spills over the top
of the shrinking ice.
Blue-faced Mr Natural takes a swig.
He inhales a nostril-full of smoky air
and coughs.
His skin feels sun-burnt. The intense lights are frazzling him.
He wishes he had sunscreen, SPF 30+, no less,
reckons he's becoming schizophrenic in his intoxication:
yawning waves babying flesh-fish
at volumes reaching the heights of silence, beckoning
rocks to roly-poly down the terra playground
and on the mountain tops, snow sloppily drops
into a cavalry charge
whilst the volcano pukes out its 3 million year old lava lunch.
Blue-faced Mr Natural stumbles home to get some sleep.
Tomorrow morning, he'll wake up with a terrible hangover
and maybe some brain damage.

Smoke Me A Tune

Holly Oreschnick

You sit at the oven
another cigarette in hand.
'Smoke me a tune' I say.
You don't hear me.
You don't see my lips not move
and the words not tumble out of my mouth.

Instead you half smile at me
and wink,
extinguish the melting effervescence,
reach to the ipod, select, dance,
then kiss me.

Kiss me deep,
so deep that I fall into the wall
become stone and dust and paint,
kiss me so deep and rough
that I scream into your mouth
and dissolve.

In an instant you are across the room
lighting up.
'Smoke me a tune' I say
as your passion leaves in a tar lit spiral
and escapes without notice
through the extractor fan.

Yawna's Tale

Mark Ellis

The princess rides the donkey as if it were a unicorn. Her prince holds the reins, leading his princess across the sand. He glances up at her and smiles. She looks down and the stern expression falls from her face, showering him like confetti. The beach, the cliffs, the ocean are all reflected in the cerulean mirror of her eyes. He winks at her and she lowers her eyes and runs her hand through donkey's mane. The prince looks out over the millpond to their right. Gulls alight from the water, their take-off accentuated by tiny rainbows as sunlight is refracted in the splashing brine. The gulls spread their wings and drift over the water's surface then ascend in the thermals rising before the cliffs, circling and cawing until they gain enough altitude and drift out over the sea.'

'You over-describe,' she says. 'I don't see it in my head. It's not true.'

'It's a fairy tale.'

'It's not true.' She looks down at him from the donkey. 'What do you think we will find?' she says.

Kubik looks up at her and shrugs, then turns his gaze towards the low rocks in the distance.

'Will we find a fallen star?' She says.

'Perhaps,' he replies. He looks up at her. 'The first gust of wind stirs the sand at their feet into a lazy vortex that disappears almost as soon as it has started.'

She shakes her head. 'Will it always be this way?' She says.

'Will what?'

She shrugs.

'The forecast is good.'

'Yes.'

He looks at the floor. 'You meant the weather?'

Yawna turns her head towards white buildings that line the

seafront.

'Yes.'

'The forecast is good.'

Yawna nods. The donkey makes a small sound and she leans forwards and strokes the top of his head. 'Shall we get ice cream?'

'Now?'

'Not now,' she says.

'Then it will be time for supper.'

'Fish then?'

'I saw a stall back there,' he says.

'And chipped potatoes?'

'Yes,' he says.

'I would like ice cream.'

'Now?'

'Yes,' she says. 'If we are to eat fish later.'

Kubik stops.

'What is it?' she says.

Kubik reaches into his pocket and pulls out a few coins.

He counts then in his hand.

She watches him from the donkey.

He looks up.

'I should have enough for both.'

'I didn't expect you to pay.'

He smiles. 'It is our day but my treat.'

Yawna nods. 'Thank you.'

Kubik holds his hand up to shield his eyes and scans the seafront. 'I don't know where sells ice cream.'

'It doesn't matter then.'

'I will go and find somewhere.'

'And I shall come.'

'No.' He says.

'But it is our day.'

'And my treat,' he says. 'You wait here, I shan't be long.'

Yawna nods. 'Help me down,' she says. 'In case the donkey bolts.'

Kubik holds up his hand and she takes it and lowers herself from her steed.

'I won't be long,' he says.

'Yes,' she says, curling her toes in the sand.

He stands there looking at her. She smiles.

'See you in a bit,' he says.

She nods.

Kubik hands her the donkey's reins then turns and sets off across the sand. The donkey turns and watches Kubik walk away.

Yawna pats him on the nose. 'Just me and you now,' she says. The donkey looks at her. Yawna smiles at him and runs her hand along the length of his ear. The donkey makes a noise like a sigh and then lowers himself into a sitting position. Yawna wraps her cardigan around herself and looks back at Kubik.

'Will it always be this way?' She says. She looks into the donkey's eyes. He blinks.

Yawna presses the sand flat with her foot and then sits down. 'Maybe not,' she says. 'Dyevushka adin,' she looks at the donkey. 'Do you know what that means?'

The donkey nuzzles the sand.

'He has always been here but not here. Sometimes I just wish...' She looks over her shoulder. 'I don't know. He could just be more...' She pushes her feet under the sand. 'Do you understand?'

The donkey stares at her.

'Yeah,' she says.

Yawna runs her hand through the sand, pushing it into a pile. She pats it down and then drops more on top of it. The donkey snorts. Yawna raises herself to her knees and heaps more sand onto the mound and pats it down. She searches the ground around her for a shell. There is one by the donkey's foot.

'Will you pass me that?' she says.

The donkey looks at her.

'Please?'

The donkey snorts, covering the shell in sand. Yawna leans across and picks up the shell. She dusts it off and then places it on top of the mound. She sits and looks at it for a moment and then squeezes some of the sand between her palms until it rises like a wall. Yawna builds the wall around the mound. She sits and stares at it and then reaches into the circle and pats two straight edges into the mound so that it is shaped like a triangle with a rounded side. Yawna places her finger on the rounded edge and then pushes it into the mound and pulls out a triangular wedge. She smoothes the sand into two arcs that meet in the middle of that edge so that it is shaped like a valentine's heart.

Yawna turns to the donkey. 'This is him,' she says pointing to the heart surrounded by the wall. 'He has a heart but he keeps it hidden.'

The donkey blinks.

Yawna curls her hand into a fist. 'And this is what I want to do to his heart,' her hand hovers above the mound.

The donkey looks towards the sea front.

Yawna brings her hand down and smashes away part of the wall. She looks at the donkey and laughs. 'I want to set his heart free,' she says. Yawna flattens the remaining part of the wall with her hand.

'Yawna,' says a voice.

She turns. Kubik is standing next to the donkey. He has an ice cream in his hand. 'Kubik,' she says.

He holds out the cone. 'Here is your ice cream.'

Yawna dusts off her hands and then takes the cone. 'Thank you.' She tastes the ice cream and then smiles. 'Delicious. Where is yours?'

'It was melting,' he says. 'I had to eat it.'

'Mine seems ok.'

'It was different,' he says. 'Mr Whippy.' Kubik looks at the floor.

Yawna licks the ice cream. 'You didn't get one.'

'I...'

'You didn't want one?'

Kubik puts his hands into his pockets. 'Yawna...'

She looks at his feet then she looks at his bowed head. 'You didn't have enough money.'

He bites his lip.

'Oh, Kubik.'

'Not if we are to eat fish for supper,' he says.

Yawna looks at her feet. She wiggles her toes in the sand.

'You want some?'
'It is for you.'
'Then it is mine to share.' She pats the sand next to her. 'Sit.'
Kubik pulls up his trousers and lowers himself onto the sand.
Yawna smiles and holds out the cone. 'Here,' she says.
He leans forwards and puts his nose above the cone. He closes his eyes as he inhales. Yawna smiles.
'It smells good,' he says.
'Taste it.'
Kubik looks at her.
Yawna winks at him.
Kubik looks at the ice cream.
'Taste it,' she says.
Kubik takes the cone between his forefinger and thumb. He smells the ice cream again then looks at her. 'Are you sure?'
Yawna nods. 'It's coffee.'
'I know.'
'Well?'
Kubik holds out the ice cream. 'I can't,' he says. 'It's yours.'
Yawna takes a handful of sand and lets it run out between her fingers.
Kubik stands holding the donkey's reins as Yawna climbs up onto the rocks. 'Be careful,' he says. 'There is seaweed.'
Yawna looks over her shoulder. 'Seaweed?' She raises her eyebrows.
'On the rocks,' he says. 'You might slip.'
'Might I?'
Kubik nods.
Yawna shakes her head and then continues to climb on the rocks. Kubik stands watching.
'Are you coming?' she shouts.
'What about the donkey?'
'Leave the donkey. Get him to wait there. He is a good donkey.'
Kubik looks at the donkey.
The donkey blinks.
'Are you a good donkey?' He says.
The donkey snorts.

Kubik pats the donkey on the head and lets go of the reins. 'Will you wait here?' He says.

The donkey turns his head to look at the sea.

Kubik kneels down and rolls his trouser leg up. He looks at the rocks, shakes his head and then rolls up his other trouser leg. He stands and walks over to the rock, places his hand on top of it and then lifts his foot into a crack. Kubik pulls himself over the rock.

'Come on,' says Yawna. She is crouching over a rock pool. 'Look there are things living here.'

'It is a rock pool,' he says. 'Of course there are things there.' He lowers himself onto his haunches at the other side of the pool and stares into the water. 'I cannot see anything.'

She does not take her eyes from the pool. 'You have to be patient.'

Kubik sighs.

'This is fun.'

Kubik stands up and puts his hands in his pockets. He turns and walks away from the pool.

'Look,' she says.

Kubik turns. Yawna plunges her arm into the water.

He frowns. 'What are you doing?'

'There is a crab.'

Kubik steps forwards and looks into the pool. 'I cannot see anything.'

Yawna draws her arm out of the water. As her hand emerges, Kubik sees that it is holding something. The crab snaps its pincers and wiggles its legs.

'Quick,' she says.

'What?'

Yawna places the crab on the rock; he snaps his pincers and then runs back towards the pool.

'No you don't,' she says placing her forefinger on the crab's back, squashing him flat.

'It will hurt if he catches you with those pincers.'

'Look at him,' she says.

Kubik walks around the side of Yawna and crouches down. 'He is mighty.'

Yawna takes her finger from the crab's back. He stands and dashes in the direction of the rock pool, enters the water with a plop. They watch as their reflections reform in the pool beneath them.

'Look,' he says. 'Young, remembered faces watch us from the pool.'

'Your words entrap your heart.' Yawna puts her hand on top of Kubik's hand. She turns to him. 'Where has the time gone?'

Kubik frowns. 'Today?'

'Our lives,' she says.

'Please Yawna.'

'When you brought me here last, there was a war. Men died for their country, for this land.'

'This land is our home.'

'But it is not where we were born.'

'Home is where you... belong.'

Yawna frowns. 'You think we belong here? You feel like this is our home?'

He nods.

'Do you know what I think?' She says.

'I have always wished that I could read your mind.'

'Home is where you stop trying,' she says.

'Do you think that I do not try?'

'You haven't tried in years.'

'I bought you an ice cream,' he says.

'When did you put a wall around your heart?' she says.

Kubik stares into the water.

Yawna sighs and gets to her feet. In the distance, there is the humming of a motor engine. Kubik frowns and then stands quickly and raises his hand to shield his eyes. 'A Lavochkin,' he says. He looks at Yawna. 'That is a Lavochkin, more than one.'

Yawna frowns.

'Look,' he says pointing at three dots on the horizon.

'Planes.'

'Fighters.'

'Here?'

'Yes. They are here.' They watch the three planes pass overhead, propellers humming. Kubik waves.

'Do you think they can see us?' He says.

'I don't know.'

Kubik waves again, continues to wave as the planes clear the tops of the houses and disappear from sight. 'They are here,' he says.

Yawna looks down into the pool. The crab watches her from behind a curtain of seaweed. 'Would you go back?'

Kubik looks at her. 'Of course.'

'Did you want to go back? All these years, have you wished you were somewhere else?'

Kubik takes her hand. She looks up at him.

'I was with you,' he says.

Yawna smiles at him and he lowers his eyes.

'Kubik,' she says.

He looks up at her.

'Thank you for a good day.'

Kubik nods. 'I love you,' he says.

The Elephant Who Came To Tea

Ami Roseingrave

Sophie sits alone in the kitchen, body shaking
like a blob of epileptic jelly, fitting helplessly
on a plate. Doorbell rings, Big Ben chiming
at ear-piercing volume in her head. It can't be
the lady next door because she pretends not to know;
even though she's lived beside her for as long as

Sophie can forget. It can't be her ex-boyfriend;
he's no more interested in her new bump than she
is. It can't be her father, he's heard there's a barring
order in place, and the locks have been changed
by a man who said he'd do the work for nothing
and then screwed her mum. Must be the psycho elephant

who used to beat up her big sister, but now makes
eyes at her. She smells his niffy pinkness seep
beneath the door. He stumbles down the hallway
and slumps into an obscure chair. Twitchier
than his cousin the tiger, who in his own way,
was almost abstemious. A Molotov with nothing less than

Bacardi 151, he hollers. Sophie pours, floats
the rum, ignites, and watches him shoot; then demands
another and lunges at her throat. Rampages through
a home of a million secret places, in search of one
more liquid fix. His pink skin livid; he chases up
and down walls in pursuit of things that only her

mind can see. A domestic rattle and hum of seismic
proportions now erupts insanities that stain walls
and windows and floors. His firebrand wretchedness

crawls beneath her clothes, her nails and skin like
maggots gorging on a body-parts picnic, or juicers
sloshing down a whitewater bender for fun. Threats

of an incursion looms terror, she drops to her knees,
begs his craving trunk to consider the innocence
in utero, and for reasons she'll never fathom, he pulls
himself together, evaporates in a puff of elephant
pink; until such time as she's feeling thirsty and not
settle for a mug of Tetley's or a flute of Darjeeling.

Swans

Jim Greenhalf

Their necks are question marks,
but they harbour no doubts about their right
to swank; on the canal they are on top.
Dipping into their dappled white
reflections is all the validation
they need. Gliding like Derby Day aristocracy,
accepting due deference
for their flying boat power and beauty.
The wingspan of Stukas and eagles,
creaming water's green surface on skis.

Things look very different from the bottom.
Down among the rotting roots of trees,
treadless trolleys and shredded tyres,
only fronded gloom is prevalent.
The light in which their elegance admires
itself does not reach this khaki habitat
of small fry and predators seeking easy prey.
Down here you must masquerade
among weeds, avoid becoming bait.
Swans win all the prizes. Swans have got it made.

Dipps, The Goose And The Gooley Goo

Timothy Allsop

I watched as he pointed the barrel of the gun at the neck of the goose. It was such an enormous creature, almost too big to be a bird. Its beak jived in and out of the corn, as it tried to make its way into the field. Its neck was as big as a man's arm. Beneath it was a massive belly which swung about. All four of us stood in silence. The goose knew we were there. It had just crossed the road in front of us. I couldn't take my eyes off it. It seemed more alive than anything I'd ever seen and I wanted to see it die.

Daniel took his time positioning his father's gun. I kept flicking my eyes to him to see if he was ready. He had this weird overhanging top lip and no chin. My dad said they were an inbred family and that's why they looked the way they did.

'Go on, then,' Darren said, his voice strained from excitement.

'Shut up. You'll scare it,' I hissed.

Dipps let out a little squeal and I had to grip his arm to make him stay quiet. He kept swaying about and then he took hold of my hand. He liked holding people's hands. I tried to pull away but he wouldn't let go. I was always amazed by how strong he was, seeing as how he was a bit of a retard and all. I was glad the others were busy watching the goose as they'd have only taken the piss.

Daniel had not said a word since he lifted the gun. He was completely still. There was something about the way he stood that reminded me of theses war films we'd been watching a couple of nights back. His finger moved onto the trigger. Even Dipps knew to keep his mouth shut. The goose seemed to know it too, for it turned and stared directly at us. It didn't make to move but stood and tipped its head to the side as if trying to talk to us. It made me wonder if what my dad said about people coming back as animals after they died was true. For a second I thought the goose might have been Mrs Taylor, who'd died last year in the house next to us. But then the goose was too old to be her. Maybe it was some great historical figure like Napoleon or Henry VIII? Or Hitler? Yes, Hitler was a good choice.

I imagined the goose had a little moustache on the end of his beak. Yeah, it was Hitler. He was a nasty man. We were about to kill Hitler.

Hitler raised its neck high and as it did I heard the shot ring through the air. I swear that sound travels faster than light when you shoot a gun. I heard it and Hitler was still standing. I'm sure of it. I felt Dipps tighten his grip. As the noise disappeared I saw the animal start to dance. It twisted round on itself like some fat snake. It didn't look like Hitler anymore. From nowhere these wings sprouted and expanded and red ribbons flew through the air. I was chewing on my lips. Dipps was screaming. He sounded like my baby brother. I tried to ignore it and focus on the goose.

By now it was a mass of flesh. Its wings were painting its belly red. I moved towards it to try and see its head. Daniel was already at the edge of the field, pulling back the corn with his hands to get a good view. Darren stood further off. He was a little small and I reckon he was scared that the bird might bite him. I felt Dipps pulling at my arm. He was bawling his eyes out. Then the bird's eyes looked directly at me. They were mad.

I could see the blood pouring from its neck, sliding down its body and onto the corn. I moved closer and was nearly at the verge when the bird pulled itself up and onto the road. Its wings smacked and smacked against the concrete. And I couldn't believe how much life was still in it.

It made a sudden squalling sound and for a moment it got mixed up with Dipps' crying. It moved along the road and fell into one of the drains at the edge of the barn. Walled in, it made a last ditch effort to escape. But very quickly it started to give up. Its wings flopped and I could see it was panting. Its body no longer seemed to be in one piece. All I could see was a bit of its neck or a leg or a bent wing. What a useless creature it was. It made me feel sad and I wanted to see it fly again. But then Daniel pointed the gun into the drain and pulled the trigger. The bird stopped moving and the echo of gunfire thinned out over the fields. We were all sweating and breathing heavily.

'That was cool that was,' Darren said in a high pitched voice.

He was fifteen and his voice hadn't broken yet. But if you ever mentioned it he'd punch you in the stomach.

'I better throw it in the bushes so my dad don't find out,' Daniel said.

He reached in and picked up the goose by its legs. It looked really heavy. He swung it towards Darren's face. Darren jumped back and told him to eff off. Daniel snorted and walked off down the lane and threw it in the bushes by the railway track which went by the farm. As he walked back it started to drizzle so we went in and played on the computer for a bit. Dipps sat quietly in a corner scratching at his lip and nibbling on a digestive biscuit. His eyes looked sore from where he'd been crying. Darren and I took it in turns to try and beat Daniel on this fighting game.
I had to breathe through my mouth cos I didn't like the smell of his house. He had really bad B.O. and he let his dogs lay on his bed. They sat their watching us with their tongues hanging out, making the room smell of fart and fust.

'You're useless at this game,' Darren said, taking the controls away from me.

I was useless. I'd never been good at computer games, except maybe Worms but that was a long while ago. I went and sat next to Dipps, who started to pull at my hair. I got out Daniel's box of toys and rummaged round. I found these old soldiers, so me and Dipps built a fort out of old shoe boxes. Daniel and Darren soon got bored and came over. Daniel took control and moved everything about. Dipps moaned and tried to put things back but Daniel gave him a clout round the head. There were times when I wanted to hit Daniel but he was bigger than me. I must admit it was cool when he brought out all these plastic trees and made a wood where the soldiers could fight each other.

The afternoon seemed to drip by. I wondered what the goose looked like all sodden and dead and lying in the bushes. The others seemed to have forgotten all about it.

I thought it might still be alive, that it might drag itself up and come and find us and peck our eyes out. When the rain finally stopped it was time for me to go home for tea but we agreed we'd meet later that evening. Daniel got this idea to go and camp out in the woods behind the school. I said I would try and nick some sausages for a barbecue.

As I wheeled my way past the railway bridge I sped up, thinking the dead goose might be lurking amongst the weeds. It was exhilarating biking out from under the bridge as there was a big hill and in seconds you could be miles away from the farm. As I reached the top Dipps caught me up on his scrappy old bike.

'You going out to the woods?'

'What do you reckon?'

'Daniel said there are wolves in the wood.'

'No, there ain't no wolves in the wood.'

'And monsters he said.'

'Go and eat your tea. I gotta get back.'

I reached the village road and peddled home. Weirdly I felt as if something was still wrong. I wanted to get home and see my dad. He was busy clearing out the shed in the back garden and I had to help him move the tools back in. I didn't like the way they hung on the wall. The chisels, the saws and the rake; they all looked as if they might fall down on top of me. I ate my tea in silence. It was a Frey Bentos pie. I don't like them, so I spent most of the time at the table, mashing through the soggy pastry with my fork until it was mush. My dad didn't seem to be too bothered. He slung his down his throat and went back to the shed. I cleared away the plates, then pinched a fiver from his wallet and went to the Co-op and bought some sausages and burgers.

The wood backed onto the primary school, wrapping its way round the school field. The easiest way to get in was to walk through the fields at the back but we never did. We always went through the school grounds. Darren would always piss in the pool. He was always getting his dick out.

It was already getting dark when we found the place where we were going to make the fire. The ground was damp from the rain and I wondered whether we'd actually be able to get the fire lit but Daniel had thought of that. He pulled out all these old newspapers and a bent tin of lighter fluid from his bag, along with some cheap looking meat and foil.

'Let's get some fire wood then,' he said.

We all started looking, kicking the scrub with our feet and slipping our bodies between thorn bushes to get at bits of dry wood. It was already getting dark and the bushes seemed to thicken and grow, snubbing out what light was left. Every now and then I'd hear Darren jumping out on Dipps, making him scream. I found myself walking away from them, trudging further into the wood. I dared myself to walk deeper into the undergrowth and as I did I began to see the monsters that lived there. They jumped out of my brain and through my ears and out onto the woodland floor, darting off behind trees, skidding under the leaves and curling up in the nettles. They were watching me, wanting me to walk further into the gloom. And then I saw the goose, except it was now three times the size and black with blood. Its eyes fixed on me. I saw it yanking my guts out. I wanted to know what it would feel like to die. In my head it was not as painful as I thought. I kind of numbed the pain so I could enjoy myself being torn apart. I almost disappeared into it – this warm melting feeling all over but then I heard the noise of shouting again.

I ran back to the others. The wood in my hands was wet from the sweat on my palms, and I felt grit in my nails. They were teasing Dipps.

'The Gooley Goo's gonna get you Dipps. That's why we brought you here. We're gonna feed you to the Gooley Goo,' Daniel said, making his voice creaky.

'Leave me alone.'

'You better run Dipps.'

'What's going on?' I said.

'We're just telling him about the monster that lives in the wood. You know about the Gooley Goo, don't you?'

Daniel cocked his head to the side and eyeballed me. I looked at him and saw that he had something in his hands. It was black and heavy looking. I thought it might be something for turning the meat in the fire but then I worked out what it was. It was his pellet gun.

'What are you going on about?' I said and laughed to try and make us all laugh. But Daniel didn't flinch. I suddenly realized that he never smiled.

'Yeah the Gooley Goo lives in the wood and he bites you on the arse. You better run or he's gonna get you,' Daniel said, pelting off into the trees.

Darren ran off into the dark and for a moment I could hear rustling and then it went quiet. Dipps came over to me and almost rested his head on my shoulder but I think he knew that even I was scared. I wondered why I ever thought it was clever to hang around these guys. I never spoke much to Daniel at school. It was only because he lived in the village.

'Come on Dipps, let's go home.'

I went to pick up my bag. I wasn't going to leave them my food to eat up. Then I heard a click, a pulse. Dipps jumped up in the air as if he had suddenly met with an invisible hurdle.

'It's the Gooley Goo,' he screeched and ran over to me.

One of the trees began to shake furiously and my tongue felt numb, like it was a bit of food in my mouth. Dipps was pulling at my hand and I felt myself gripping on tightly. A creepy squalling noise like the goose in its last moments came echoing through the dark and again I could see the bird with red eyes coming at me.

'Let's get out of here,' I said and we started to run through the trees which seemed to swallow our steps.

There was more clicking and I thought I heard a tree tut as we passed it. Dipps was crying. My eyes were wet from the cold.

'Aggh,' a voice growled.

We stopped dead.

'One of you has to make a sacrifice to the Gooley Goo.' It was Daniel. He came out of the darkness, as if he was made from it. The pellet gun in his hands was pointed directly at us.

'The Gooley Goo will let us go if one of you gives some blood. You better choose quickly,' he said.

'Don't, don't, don't. I want to go home,' Dipps whined.

'Daniel just stop it, all right?'

Daniel pointed the gun at my chest.

'You better choose whether it's you or him, cos I'm gonna have to shoot one of you. We can't all die.'

I felt myself starting to sob, even though I was telling myself not to. I closed my eyes and saw feathers burst out of my skin and then I was twisting. I couldn't breathe and whenever I opened my mouth little spurts of blood arched out from my throat. My muscles ached and felt as if they were being sucked dry. I opened my eyes. I was holding Dipps in front of me. I'd hooked my arms around his and I was telling him to shut up and that it wouldn't hurt. I saw Daniel point the gun at Dipps' arse and fire. Dipps let out a wail and started to howl. His body went all soft. He slid down my legs and curled up onto the floor.

Daniel sneered and walked off back towards the camp.

'Come on, get up,' I said.

Dipps just kept sobbing. I wanted to look at where Daniel had hit him. I leaned down and pulled at his trousers. There was a bit of blood and a little bruise where the pellet had hit; it was no bigger than a Smartie. It didn't look that bad. Dipps kept crying. I pulled him up and tried to take his hand but it was limp. He started to walk away back towards the school field. I followed him. We got to the fence.

'Wait for me,' I said.

He turned and looked at me and didn't say anything. He was still shaking and I noticed his trousers looked damp. A bit of me wanted to hurt him, to see how much more he would cry.
I didn't. He sniffed and climbed over the fence and walked off across the field and into the darkness. I climbed over and tried to head in the same direction. But he was gone. I sat down on the grass. It was pitch black apart from a few pimpled stars and a single security light on the side of the school. I lay out and pretended that I was the goose, dying in the drain. I held my breath and waited in the hope that something would come along and kill me. But nothing did.

Conjuror

Karl O'Neil

A coronary convert to living, you almost looked funny
as you pushed yourself to a brisk pace up the road,
the once pedal-tapping feet now stamping the concrete
in a shivering panic to sustain a chord of life.

What was the point? Soon you were back in the company
of Mick McQuade, rubbing the leaves of the forbidden plant
between your stubby fingers, so inflamed already with arthritis
that the piano was sold and all music locked away.

I tried to give you back the legacy of notes and love
of music you instilled in me, but I should have known
you didn't need to walk around listening to tapes
to hear the three Bs buzzing in your head.

Still you could paint, and I remember sitting for you
in a caravan in Mullaghmore during the Twelfth holiday
and being told my real father was a pedlar named Delaney
who would take me back if I was a bad boy.

You jested, of course, as you always did.
(That's a second thing I inherited from you,
a peculiar sense of humour, where nothing is sacred
unless you can joke about it.)

You painted me well, catching my permanent
dopey dreamlike state and mass of blonde curls,
neither of which you would claim as your gift. No,
my placid temperament, intelligence, and easy ear,
you vowed as your own, in your usual modest way.

One thing I didn't absorb was your love of fishing,
and I think you preferred to be left alone,
squatting in contemplation by the bank of a river,
thumb and forefinger stroking midge-repellent pipe,

mind humming Elgar,
eyes pinned to the tip of a rod
(which never dips)
until the lights fade

and I leave you,
my wading father,
Edwardian conjuror,
silhouette of tweed.

Paper Flowers

Julie Mellor

She bought crepe paper from the Post Office,
cut bands of colour that stretched like lengths
of intestine, sweated pink in our snatching hands.
She rolled the strips into buds, nipped them tight,
fronded them to petals, carnations blossoming
from her finger tips, a garrotte of cotton to stop them
unfurling. Spring bloomed on the sagging settee,
one bar of the fire on for a show of heat.
When he belched his way through the door
she swept them into a carrier bag and hid them
behind her back. We used to knock at neighbours'
houses, asking ten pence for a bunch of three.
Some nights I still dream of flowers, stab wounds
blooming through her Chelsea Girl blouse.

Unicorns Don't Have Wings

Kyrill Potapov

This is not a metaphor. This is before I knew what a metaphor was.

Imagine a frayed string of liquid which spread across the soft back of an armchair, and sang in staccato as it hit the bright linoleum. Imagine young threads of liquid flowing acrobatically to the door and the TV. Imagine moth-eaten blinds working under the misconception that they could stop the heat of the sun. The air was slow enough to taste, sour. Imagine a soft heap of cotton supporting two naked legs.

I don't know why but DIVORCE was in the bathroom. When a train passed I had to hold still to stop the SPIES from seeing me. DIVORCE had SPIES to make sure everything was safe and even that clementines were eaten one segment at a time.

My granddad kept jars. From the kitchen, when the sun was right, they looked like cartoon characters. Some were fat with white tops and some were like cucumbers. They stood in rows on the dusty tiles of the balcony. My mum often asked what the empty jars were for and he replied 'We'll see.'

I think he knew about the spies too. I often hid the jars. I'd find them when I yanked a sweater out of the wardrobe or in the freezer or rolled up in the big carpet that's standing in the corner of the living room. Sometimes I put things in the jars.

Apricot makes blue mould and carrot makes brown mould and chicken makes black mould and hair makes no mould and milk goes solid like plastic.

It was also fun to drop jars from the balcony and watch them explode like ink on paper. One day a woman who smelled of milk and leaves had come round to tell my granddad that someone from the tenth floor was trying to kill her. She said her leg had been shredded by glass shards. Her legs looked fine.

I got the bus to the metro station with my granddad and took

the train to a stop I'd never heard of. We walked along a broad road to a tree-filled valley. We walked down the stone steps and around a tall wooden fence. There was a church on the other side of the fence and another building like a supermarket. A man came and took me to a room with other children. My granddad left. I played Tetris and then my mum came. I played Tetris on the tube home and my mum was annoyed that I wasn't crying.
I went back there the next day, and the next.

Then, my mum came home with a man who spoke like he had food in his mouth. He had a big bag with him and gave my mum soaps and gave me a big marzipan pig and stickers with donkeys on them. I asked her what the stickers were for and she said that some things were harder to buy now than before.
I asked my granddad what the stickers were for and he said, 'we'll see'.

I stuck them to the window by the balcony. When I came back to the living room, the man with the weird voice knelt down and breathed on me.

'You know, you're a Bolshevik. You're Mikhail Gorbachev.'

Things made a lot more sense from then on.

A slanted pane of light shone across my mum's face and illuminated her ear, nose and mouth. She clasped her wrist in the shadows with her other hand and breathed loudly. She was singing. She tilted back and forth without moving her feet and sang a high and unsteady 'Huuuuh.' I still hadn't pulled my trousers up or jumped off the armchair. My eyes were losing focus and all I could see was a nose bobbing gently up and down like a yacht, blowing its foghorn.

My cat hid slippers. I'd find them on a crossword puzzle in the newspapers under the mirror in the hall, under the fridge or wedged between jars. Sometimes he would bring me a slipper and not like the dogs with their sticks but like it was important. He knew when there was someone at the door before they had rung the doorbell. He sat on top of wardrobes and jumped on people's heads. He purred slowly so that the chairs shook. He knew so much and helped me so much. I don't think anybody knows what it's like to have a cat for a dad.

Everyone said I discontinued the politburo. Here is what that means:

I remember hugging my knees in the woods by my school, then saying 'let's play holes' without knowing what it means, still not knowing. I hadn't expected other kids to ask me how to play. Soon there were many kids, all quiet and waiting to play. I told them that 'holes' meant we had to dig a hole into the big oak on the hill. In the middle of the oak was another world or an animal like a unicorn. Next lunch time we all stole forks from the canteen.

My dad came home sideways, or backwards or with his photographer equipment covering his face. Sometimes he'd be standing backwards outside the door and my mum would open the door and shout at him but I liked it. My dad smelled of leather and petrol and the thing you rub under your nose to stop the snot. He gave me Vasya, my cat. I came home and Vasya was there and my granddad was in the kitchen and wouldn't come out until mum made him a cup of tea and a black bread and cheese sandwich and locked Vasya in my room. When my granddad came out of the kitchen I could hear him muttering 'we'll see' outside my door, I promise.

My dad was from Astrakhan where there are real eagles and watermelons and fish swim in people's baths. My dad wasn't allowed to smile because he would get arrested if people saw his teeth. My dad took photos for newspapers every day. The only photos in our house were of people who are dead. He once took a photo of my hands for a magazine. I don't like having my photo taken. My dad taught me to kick my leg higher than my head so that if villains came I can attack them. He went and learned Aikido with his other sons but I wasn't allowed to go.

When my dad was home he acted like a cat. He rolled around on the floor all the time and he sat in the lotus position and he rolled balls across the floor and he lay on his back because of the photographer equipment and he ate cat food except when Vasya did it I was allowed to play with him. He also prayed to God, and that sounded like Vasya talking or purring. My dad also took me to a church in Astrakhan and got me Christened which means I have to wear a necklace with a cross on it and that my dad's dad will show me how to catch fish.

My dad came home sideways and shook hands in the hall with the man with food in his mouth. Mum was annoyed.

Here is how I knew when mum was annoyed:

She would tilt her chin up and look at my hair or my ear when talking to me. She would talk about her God. She would laugh with her mouth but not with her eyes. She would iron my socks. She would listen to the radio. She would open a door if it was closed and close it if it was open. We would have rice and meat for dinner. She would say 'I am annoyed' loudly.

Mum asked if she can talk to dad in their room and the man with food in his mouth said he would phone my mum and left, also sideways. Mum went to her room but dad stayed in the hall and asked me what I had done today. I said that I had been at school learning Swedish. I actually didn't like Swedish and also did maths and art and writing but dad liked it when I said I did Swedish. Mum grabbed dad by the elbow and led him down the hall. Dad gripped me round the wrist and dragged me with him. I tried to run ahead and grab my mum's other hand but then my dad let go of me and my mum let go of him. My mum put her hand on my shoulder and faced my dad.

'He is a good Christian boy,' my dad said.

And then it was like I could never complete the circle. It was like my dad had grabbed me for his own keeping so that I couldn't escape. He gave me a gift that I couldn't even see well enough to hide. Not like a jar. I still couldn't catch a fish. Christian was a threat. My mum laughed and looked at his hair. I AM MIKHAIL GORBACHEV.

* * *

The oak was soft and wet and easy to dig into. Three of us climbed up the hill. We used forks and sharp sticks and a knife to dig into the tree. Bark fell in bits like Lego bricks and disappeared in all the leaves. There were many ants on the tree. Sometimes I built a house for the ants out of sticks or fern. Martha Petrovna said I was allowed to kill ants because they didn't have souls. I decided that all the ants could come into the hole when I finished digging. Digging was hard because you had to be really strong to do it and the forks kept breaking.

Here is what Pasha said which upset me:

'Unicorns don't have wings.'

* * *

There was a long table in my parent's bedroom with a mirror at the back that lit up if you pulled a cord down the side. The table was covered in my dad's photographer equipment and some CDs. It was mostly jars. They were not like my granddad's jars. These jars were completely black and heavy, light couldn't shine through them. I wasn't allowed to touch them. Some of the jars had grey caps, those jars were for films and I had to put them in the fridge when my dad had filled the film with photos.

When my dad was annoyed he would go and roll around on the floor like a cat. I hated his jars. I didn't see why he didn't let me hide them because he always said how they made his back hurt and that's why mum shouted at him, because he always said that his back hurts.

My mum took her hand off my shoulder and walked into her room. We slowly followed. She came up to the table in her room and swept everything on it onto the floor. Some of the jars flew into the wall before they fell on the floor. Nobody said anything. My mum ran into the toilet and my dad walked out the door, straight on. I looked at the jars on the floor. Now that they weren't next to the mirror, it looked like there weren't as many of them. One of the big jars had opened and I went over to look at what was inside of it. Then my mum screamed so loudly that I dropped that jar and it fell again and whatever was inside sounded like it had broken. I ran into my room and found the matchbox I had stolen from my granddad. I tipped out all the matches into my drawer. I took off my necklace and put it in the matchbox. I took the matchbox and was going to throw it out of my window but the SPIES would see me. I threw it on top of my wardrobe instead.

Vasya was clever because when he was hungry he would lie on his back and pretend to be dying of hunger. He got so fat that he couldn't walk through the legs of the stool in the kitchen. My dad put carrot and fish porridge in his bowl but he never ate it, he was smarter than that. Vasya knew that my granddad had a bad appetite. He would wait until my granddad finished lunch or dinner and tipped the food he didn't eat into Vasya's bowl. The same lump of carrot and fish porridge would sometimes be in his bowl for a week. My dad said Vasya wasn't allowed to eat the food that the cats on the television ate. My mum always bought food that humans on the television ate but never the cat food. My dad made carrot and fish porridge for himself too. Our kitchen was blue and smelled of carrot and fish porridge, milk and garlic.

I had many books but I didn't like reading. I had one big book with a desert island on the front cover. There was a ship and the desert island had a jungle and a house or a palace on it. I couldn't read the book because it was in English. My mum read the book to me but I didn't understand it because it was in English. My granddad read fairy tales to me.

My dad was sitting in the armchair with a thin textbook in one hand. The sun was too bright for me to see its pages. He asked me how to say 'lion' in English. I really didn't know but I pretended that I knew. I told him I needed to go to the toilet and ran over to my mum's room and my mum whispered to me what the answer was from her bed where she was also reading something. I ran back and told my dad and he was really surprised that I knew it. He asked me how to say 'tiger' and I had to run back again but he still didn't know I was cheating. Then he asked me how to say 'cat' but I really did know how to say that.

I could smell the gingerbread in the oven. Dad had bought sour cream and strawberries to put on the gingerbread but still hadn't taken them out of the bag. But that's not how it follows. My bedroom was also the living room.

The first time someone did something evil to me, when I hadn't even done anything evil to them first, was in school. An older boy dragged me out of the classroom window and held me hanging by my neck. Couldn't kick him or anything, didn't even tell anyone (until now). Now we're even.

That was the day that we found a treasure. I didn't actually find it but I told people that I did. Someone found a tyre and inside the tyre was a black bag and in the bag were loads of stones, all different colours, all looking different in the sunlight. There was gold and diamonds and about a dozen others. Martha Petrovna said that they were crystals. I said that we should give them all to the church next to our school so that they can rebuild it. We kept a piece of treasure each to take home and gave the rest to a woman who was sitting in the church. She asked if we were from the school and we said we were and she said that she'll make sure the priest gets all the rocks.

When I got home my mum and granddad sat me down and told me that my rock would give me cancer. I didn't see how a rock can give you a disease. They made me throw it away.
I threw it out of the window but nothing happened when it hit the ground. None of the other children's parents told them that the rocks would give them cancer. Pasha's parents let him get the tube home alone and play Doom on his computer. I didn't even have a computer.

But CRASH. From the kitchen I see my mum on the balcony. My dad is lying in shards of glass – broken jars. His forehead is bleeding. My granddad is standing behind me looking at my dad and shaking.

'There it is, you see, there it is.'

My mum says that my dad is a monk now. Monks aren't allowed to have children so my dad has to pretend he doesn't have me.

'Why did I have a child? You're not my child, you are your father's child.'

My cross is in my matchbox. I am no-one's child. I am INVISIBLE.

Vasya and I climbed onto my wardrobe and grabbed the box of matches. I can't remember how far into the oak we got.
I don't know if we had decided that we'd dug far enough or if children just got bored of playing and found new games. There were older and taller kids all around me. A game that the older kids played was to jump from the hill to the roof of a coal power station. The coal power station was a little building with rats in it. It was dangerous to jump onto it. What I did instead was to take the petrol can under the church steps and run to the old

oak and to throw petrol into the hole. I took out my matchbox and some matches and dragged two matches at the same time against the matchbox then threw the lit matches into the hole. I ran down the hill, away from everyone. I ran to where the hill dropped off into concrete. I stood facing the coal power plant. I jumped, fell.

Sitting with a sling in the sour smelling armchair I saw it all. My mum bought me a pickled onion and that was the first time I had tasted a pickled onion. She also bought me an origami book but I already knew how to make most of the models in it. My mum stood crying with her arms in a lotus position. She was looking at a piece of card on the wall that I had drawn on. It had two women crossing a bridge on it. My dad was kneeling on the floor, putting his jars and some socks into a big brown rucksack. My dad was crying as well. My mum shouted at me because I was rolling my eyes which is where I look at the ceiling but don't know why I'm doing it. My legs were covered in white paper. My dad said that he will see me again and I say OK and give him this:

[Stick Origami Crane Here]

And then he left.
    We went back to my school with my mum. We walked in silence along the broad road until we came to the stone steps. There it was: the oak. It was half black and slanted. It had much bigger holes in it. There was a big chunk missing in the middle. Little black threads flew off it, into the sky. It was like a black ant on a flower; with its antennas and its bent legs. We never walked down those stone steps. After that, we went to England. It was strange to see the oak still smouldering. I think that was when I grew up: when I realised that I could turn away from something and it will still be there when I look back.

Buying Into The Property Market

Skye Loneragan

The SOLD sticker
straddling FOR SALE
is peeling in the drizzle.

My heart is curling
just the same
at the thought of having to own something
to keep the rain
off my hair.

I will sit here and stare
at my latest purchase
before unpacking the banana boxes.

House Clearance

Gaia Holmes

Slowly she's clearing things out
starting with the useless items:
chipped china cups,
trust shot-through with hairline cracks,
orphaned plugs and fuse wire,
the dead stereos
he'd planned to resurrect.

And then there are the things
she'd like to keep
but knows she'll never use:
those bright, rich nights
that no longer fit,
the creaking songs
of the bed frame
now dull and flat
and out of key,
the sugared lovers' lingo
that has settled like cobwebs
in the corners of the room,

and love, what's left of it,
she boils up the bones,
flavours the vapid broth
with stock and spice,
sets up a soup shack
on the ragged edge of town
and serves it to the homeless,
the hungry, the loveless creatures
of the night.

Blessed

Gaia Holmes

Your grandmother
had tins full of prayer tags
and soft Garibaldi biscuits.
She kept gossip like hymn sheets
folded into the back
of her breeze-block bible,
kept a row of icons
above her fireplace
with garish hearts
like rotting plums,
reserved the best bone china,
for priests, saints
and other visitations.

If you were lucky, upon leaving
you'd be blessed with a dry kiss
pressed upon the brow,
otherwise you'd leave
drenched in a frenzy of spit,
Hail Mary's and Holy water.

You said I'd done quite well,
made a good impression
but I could tell by the way
she edged her way
around my name
and how damp I was
when we said goodbye
that she thought
I'd burn in Hell.

Vanilla Grave Dirt

Christopher Parvin

Heat has a smell. It can be stinking swamps or baking earth, grass fires or hot drains. Today it is a cook pot of sweat and heated dust, hot leather bibles and stale lily of the valley. A rank, almost animal smell, which makes the preacher's sermon unseemly.

Daisy is sitting by the doors, the large scarred wood is propped open with bricks and the lightest breeze pulls at the twists of hair poking from under her sun hat. Yet still her mother sleeps. It is easy for her to creep away.

Blue Kill is a simple town. A home for good country folk, people who will sit on their porches and tip their hats at strollers on summer nights, or take coconut cream pie for christenings and fried catfish for funerals. It's been three weeks but Daisy's house still smells of catfish.

The screen door is open, anchored by a cast iron cow from their aunt Nancy two towns over. Daisy's mother hates it. Her grandmother Cleo thinks it's cute as anything and says so, frequently. She is home when Daisy arrives, shelling peas in front of the wireless.

'Your mamma know where you are?' Her question isn't harsh and Daisy only shrugs. Cleo chuckles low and husky. 'She'll slap the black off you yet girl, better make yourself scarce before church lets out.'

'Can I go visit granddaddy?' Daisy asks too brightly.

'Well alright then, but don't stay there too long hun. The snakes might be lazy in the heat but they're sure not stupid.'

Daisy grins at the tired warning and runs through the house to the kitchen. She waits until she hears the pit pit of peas hitting copper before she takes her hidden supplies in shaking fingers. She leaves through the back door.

When the big city needed a water supply they came in their

hundreds and dug through the riverbed, diverting the flow. It left behind a deep groove – like a scar on the land – and a lot of pale butter coloured ground. Out of the way, hidden by bent sycamores it is perfect for a graveyard. They buried Daisy's grandfather in the vanilla grave dirt at the beginning of summer. It had been hot then too.

The sand is so dry it's almost like dust and Daisy's black Sunday shoes cloud grey before she reaches the grave. Stood in front of the simple wooden marker she lets her Hessian bag drop. There is a moment of hesitation, the briefest of doubts before she opens the drawstring.

The bundled chicken feet are hard and scaly, yet warm to the touch and the jar of chicken blood deathly cold. Cleo told her the spell during a power out and she remembers her grandmother intoning the steps in her gravelly voice. That had caused the biggest fight of them all, her mother red as a snapper as she yelled herself hoarse. She doesn't hold with magic.

The blood is poured on the grave with the feet in her dominant hand. She has to step just right, and coax the dead back to the surface with whispers.

'Granddaddy can ya hear me?' Daisy half expects a reply and when one doesn't come her confidence shakes.

'I'm pig sick to do this to you, after grandma spent so much hiring that choir to sing. When I get to heaven, I'm gonna rest a while – that cost her dear that did – but it's those men from the city. Granddaddy they're coming back and the town can't think of a thing to do about it. They wanna get rid of Blue Kill, throw it out like so much bad cornbread. You were always the smartest man in Blue Kill, everybody says it, if anyone could think of a way to help us it'd be you. So I'm really sorry to disturb your sleep, really I am, but we'd all be real grateful if you'd pay us a visit.'

There is silence, the birds stop humming gospel, the breeze dies. Daisy leans forward until the vanilla dirt brushes her ear.

'Why are you bothering the dead on a hot day like this? Make you faint that will.'

Her scream echoes as a sharply dressed man steps from the tree line.

'Who the hell are you?'

'Good question. I've been known as someone who can help, if only I know the problems.' He wears a white cotton suit with harsh creases down each leg, and a salt and pepper beard over a ragged jaw.

'You're not from around here. My mamma says I shouldn't talk to strangers, they only have one thing on their minds.'

'And what's that sweetie?'

Daisy shrugs.

'What if I told you I can solve any problem you have without you needing to intrude on your good granddaddy's well earned rest?'

Her eyes narrow. 'How'd you know he's my granddaddy mister?'

'Why I used to play poker with him, out at old Albert's place. You know old Albert?'

Daisy smiles. The free smile of the trusting. 'He used to give me cough candy.'

'Well what do you know?' The man produces a piece of scarlet sweet from his blazer pocket and hands it over. Daisy sucks it with relish.

'They're going to bulldoze the town, wanna build a road right through. No one here has a car – not a working one anyways – no one but Mr Hank from the food store, what do they wanna road for?'

He twists his face with pity and concern. 'There are bad men in the world sweetie, very bad men.'

'What's your name?'

'Call me Lou.'

'I'm Daisy.'

'Are you hot Daisy?' She nods and wipes non-existent sweat from her forehead to emphasize her point.

'Come on, let Uncle Lou buy you a coke.'

The dusty Main Street – in all its shades of magnolia – is like a ghost town with everyone still entombed in the church. Daisy tugs at Lou's sleeve.

'Mr Hank is in church mister, we'll have to wait.'

'But I'm a friend of Mr Hank's too Daisy, he left me a key.'

The key comes from the same pocket as the candy. Thanks

to the big freezer by the far wall the air in the store is cooler than outside, almost comfortable.

'Right. One coke coming up.'

'Can I have a black cow instead?'

'Sure can.' He adds a scoop of ice cream to the glass and watches it froth.

'You said you can help with the city folk?'

'That's my business Daisy, but I can't do it for nothing. It's gonna cost me a lot to fix this town for good.'

'I don't have any money.'

'Oh honey, I want your soul not money.'

Daisy's eyes go wide and her mouth hangs open. 'Oh no, you can't have that mister, I need my soul.'

'Whatever for?' Daisy only shrugs. 'See, why would you want to clutter yourself up with things you don't use? Tell you what, I'll only take it in thirty years, how does that sound? When your thirty-eight you'll come back here and give it to me. I can't say better than that.'

'Not a day earlier?'

'Nope.'

'And you'll keep the town safe?'

'It'll never change, promise.'

Daisy sips her drink and thinks.

'Deal.'

Daisy all but runs home, a grin threatening to crack her face. People dot the streets, fanning themselves with those hand held bibles with floppy leather covers. Each face that turns and smiles in greeting makes Daisy's heart beat harder. She'd saved them all. In her excitement she trips on Nancy's door stop, her knee scraping across the unwaxed floor. A necklace of blood oozes on her skin.

'Damn it,' she hisses.

'You see what I mean?' Her mother shouts. She stands towering over Cleo's pea shelling form, the white glove of one hand stained scarlet. An empty pickle jar sits on the window sill.

'Blasphemies just fall out of the girl. This is your fault, filling her head with your...'

'Bessie Louise Harper remember who you are talking to,'

Cleo whispers. At once Bessie's voice drops to match her mother's.

'You teach the girl witchcraft, all this hoodoo stuff. Mamma it's not natural, I can't have my Daisy growing up a devil child.'

'Like me you mean?' Cleo doesn't glare, she shells peas.

'I didn't mean that!'

An uncomfortable silence falls. Daisy lets the blood build on her knee staring at her mother in shock.

'I saved the town,' her voice is small compared to the silence and almost goes missing. Cleo's sharp eyes snap in her direction.

'Come here, I'll see to your knee, your mamma can get the iodine,' with a huff Bessie storms into the kitchen.

'What did you mean just now child, you saved the town?'

Her excitement rekindled Daisy beams.

'I sure did. I made a deal with Lou, he's gonna keep the town safe forever.'

'Who's Lou honey?'

'Well I was trying to bring granddaddy back see?' Her eyes dart to the empty jar but she dare not move her head. 'When Lou showed up, he said if I give him my soul he'll save the town.'

'Your soul? You don't want your soul?'

'Yep, but he's only gonna take it in thirty years! I'll never get that old'. Cleo struggles with the childish logic but Bessie returns.

'Mamma, I've decided. I'm going to take Daisy to live with Nancy. She has farm land, it'll be a nice place for her to grow up.'

To Daisy's surprise Cleo nods.

'It might be for the best.' The iodine stings Daisy's knee, the sickly scent tickling her nose.

'But I don't wanna go.'

'I went by the graveyard after church, I found your... things,' Bessie thunders, 'I don't think you have much choice in the matter. What were you thinking?'

'Leave the girl be, she knows she did wrong.'

'Leave her..? Fine. I'm going to use the pastor's telephone to call Nancy.'

Once Bessie had gone Cleo pulled Daisy onto her lap, her expression solemn.

'I love you, you know that don't you?'

Daisy nods. 'Are you mad I tried to talk to granddaddy?'

'Oh no sweetheart,' Cleo's age warped hands, all knuckles and brown skin, strokes Daisy's hair. 'Now you listen, don't you go saying anything to your mamma about Lou, let that be our little secret. You can go stay with your aunt Nancy for a while, she has cows, you'll like them, and I'll see that what has to be done is done.'

Daisy nods hazily.

'I won't let Lou have you, you're mine understand?'

Daisy is asleep.

* * *

Sometimes I wake in the middle of the night and think about the day I left Blue Kill. It's all sepia coloured now. From the safety of New Orleans I can believe it's not real.

I don't know why I've not been back. I get a birthday card from my Grandmother every year and letters every couple of weeks acting as detailed newspapers, mapping the life and times of the town and people I can hardly remember. Even when I don't respond she doesn't give up. This year she's asked me to visit.

'Mom it's okay, I'm only staying for a few days. I still think of her as family even if you don't.'

'It's our own life, you can do what you want. I just want to know if you've considered my offer.' Bessie's bitterness crackles down the line.

I jump the last few steps of the stairs and sit at the kitchenette table. The imitation granite is chipped in places, a small puckered burn from a candle black in the centre. I pick at it as my fiancee makes pancakes.

'We don't want to live in New England mom, Marcus moved to America to get away from that.' I roll my eyes as he slips a plate in front of me.

'Once you're married you'll need a good house to set up a family, there is lots of work in Boston.'

'That's the joy of being a writer, I can work almost anywhere.'

'Just think about it, that's all I ask.' Bessie hangs up and I dig into my pancakes.

'She only cares about you,' Marcus starts.

'No, she thinks the only reason someone would marry me is if I were pregnant and she wants the non-existent baby to have a big house.'

'That's something to think about.'

I stare at him, those dimples.

'When I get back, we'll talk.' We kiss over the maple syrup. A car horn blasts from the street. 'Damn it, that'll be my taxi'.

'Sure you don't want me to come? I'd love to meet your family.' Marcus is sweet, giving me those puppy dog eyes.

'It's only my grandma living there now, you'd be bored shitless.' He offers me an exaggerated sigh. 'I'll be back in a few days, well before my birthday, then you'll have me all to yourself.'

'Are you going to invite her to the wedding?'

'Already have, I'll get her reply while I'm down there. Now go, my taxi is waiting.'

'Love ya sugar,' he tries in a southern accent. I prefer his crisp English but he will try.

'Love you too.'

I grab my travel bag from the hall and bound down the steps to the street. The air is muggy, drifts of litter already forming around the taxi's dusty black belly.

'Harper?' He calls from the front seat. I know most of the drivers in town but this guy is new.

'That's right.' I slide onto the moth eaten seats and instantly wind down a window.

As we pull away under the caramel coloured columns supporting our apartments I can't help but think it won't be Harper for much longer. I grin like a child.

The drive seems endless, ferried down the country by one of those rare taxi drivers that doesn't speak beyond asking you your name and destination. I can tell he's not used to going this far south. Despite his vest he's already sweating, his fingers slipping from the wheel every once in a while and we're not even in prime haze country yet.

'So what's your name?' I try. His head twitches as if I slapped his bald scalp, but he doesn't answer. 'Fine,' I mutter.

We leave the well-maintained highways and stumble into country back lanes just as the sun hits mid-day. He's using a road that follows the old riverbed. It's closed in land and the heat is oppressive, mix that with the sway of the cab and I start to feel my breakfast clawing at the walls of my stomach. My eyes focus on the crucifix swinging from the rear view mirror. It doesn't help.

'I'm sorry, I think you'll need to pull over.' He turns to face me. His pupils are wide, sweat pools in his eyebrows and pours down his fleshy cheeks. He doesn't look well himself. 'Please, I'm going to be sick.'

The colour drains from his face but he does as I suggest, I stagger out onto sandy ground. My vomit is sour and makes my eyes water.

'I don't know what's wrong with me, I normally travel so well.' I look up and frown. 'Where the fuck are we?'

'I'm sorry about this madam, I really am, but she says it's for your own good.'

'What are you talking..?' The driver has a shotgun pointing at my head.

'Look if this is about money, it's all in my purse,' I point back to where the long strap of my bag dangles from the open door, 'See? On the back seat?'

He looks like a dog chewing a hornet.

'I wouldn't do this for money, God's mercy no. Cleo said I had to do this, I had to, ain't no two ways about it. Save that girl she said.'

'Cleo who?'

He doesn't want to answer, I can see it in the trembling fat on his neck. I don't understand. Who...

'You mean my grandmother?'

'Yes madam.'

'My grandmother told you to kill me? You're fucking crazy!' I turn to run.

'Don't you run!' It's almost a shriek, 'I'll hunt you down, I was told to get you before your birthday and that's just what I'll do!'

I run.

The undergrowth is thick and dry, snapping a trail of tinder there's no chance I'll lose him. My stomach churns, adrenalin hindering as much as helping. I trip once and feel his meaty hand grip my ankle. I kick out hard, twisting on the parched ground until I connect with something soft. He backs off but doesn't drop. It gives me a few minutes but spears of pain shoot up from my foot and stab my hip.

I limp through a corpse and stand my ground. He approaches slowly quaking as if fresh from an electric chair. The shot gun jitters in his hand, the other is held steady by the cross at his throat.

'Please don't,' I try my best to hold my voice steady, 'Please.'

'It's for the best. She said to say some things. That the whole town is real grateful, really they is but... but no kin of hers is going to the big pit. That she loves you, and will see you soon. I'm sorry.'

My gut revolts, I can't face him. I hear the shot with my back to him. I taste the copper in my throat. I recognize the vanilla ground rushing nearer.

* * *

Cleo Harper shells peas on her porch. The boards, long overdue a coat of white wash, golden in the fading sunlight. A sharply dressed man walks up the few worn steps and tries to take a seat next to her on the swing. Her hand snaps out, slaps his knuckles. Lou stays standing.

'You win,' he says simply.

'I guess so.'

The peas in the battered copper bowl rot and mould, a black mass of fertilizer smelling of shit and decay. Lou sneers, tips his hat and leaves.

Cleo smiles through her tears.

Travel Writing

Ian McMillan

I opened the drawers and closed the drawers
in the bedroom in the B&B. I made use
of the tea and coffee-making facilities
and I created a small sculpture from the packets
of milk and sugar. The landlady is a flower arranger
and she's just off to her class. That's her car
you can hear driving away up the lane. You can still
hear it. You can still hear it. You can still hear it. You
can still hear it. You can... no, now you can't.
In case of fire I should leave the building: there will be sparks,
I guess. Sparks that could be described in the third, no,
fourth paragraph of the piece I'll be writing.
If I could find my pen.
I am so effing jeffing lonely.
Arrange that.

A Room To Write In

Gillian Davis

My room is open plan.
Rain or shine,
huddled in an anorak
or nude
I'll find inspiration.

My room's south coast
has grockles,
sunny beaches,
deckchairs,
Punch and Judy parents.
This wall is decorated with shells.

My room's east coast
has a lighthouse,
a defeated moon,
jagged rocks,
worried wives in cloaks.
This wall is decorated with driftwood.

My room's north coast
has celebrities,
mansions,
fairy lights,
prowling paparazzi.
This wall is decorated with 'Hello'.

My room's west coast
has dunes,
wild winds,
gulls,
the horizon.
This wall is blank for thinking.

The Citizens

Louis Malloy

Werner drank more hot wine, slammed the cup down on the table and made himself laugh hard like the others. There were five of them sitting down, ignoring the absence of a sixth, all with their anoraks and ski boots still on. Werner laughed but he didn't say much. No-one said much apart from Max, who sat at the centre of the table and was the focus of the group.

'A toast to Anita,' shouted Max.

'Yes! Anita!'

The other men repeated her name, until the woman in the small kitchen behind the bar came out, carrying a hand towel.

'Come on my beautiful. My beautiful hostess!'

Max made to put his arm around her waist, but the woman slipped easily away and then put the towel over his head and rubbed his hair.

'Oh, you want to give me a bath? Shall we? Shall we bathe together tonight Anita?'

There was more laughter and Werner watched the woman raise an eyebrow and maintain a slight smile.

'To Anita,' they all shouted.

She took a delicate bow and went back to the kitchen.

'She'll do for me,' said Max in a much lower voice. He looked around the table and winked. 'She's done for me before.'

There was a different sound now, a low moan of approval. Werner doubted that Max had ever been with Anita, but he wasn't sure. Maybe he could get what he wanted, even a woman like that who knew how to deal with the big men, with the heavy drunks. So Werner tapped the table along with the others in applause of Max's claims. Then they drank more wine and took some meat from the plate in the middle of the table and continued the companionable afternoon. Werner breathed in the tobacco smoke and kept drinking. He was tired, not having slept for more than a few hours during the previous three nights. He wondered how everyone else had slept and how much he would have to drink to get to sleep that night. As he tried to get his body to relax, Max started shouting again.

'Who wants to hammer in a nail?'

'Yes!'

However worried they might have been, they all shouted and laughed and Werner could see no sign of doubt in anyone's expression, just the joy of an afternoon out on the mountain with their friends. They zipped up their anoraks and pulled on their hats and went outside.

There was a tree stump in front of the hut, used for a drinking game which involved nothing more than hammering in nails with the narrow side of a claw-hammer. They gathered around and looked at the surface of the trunk, much of which was covered with hundreds of nail heads. Werner half-closed his eyes so that the nails became one sheet of metal glimmering in the low afternoon sun. He had played the game here before and at the other huts on the mountain, always slightly drunk and until now always happy to be spending time in this useless pursuit.

One of the men picked up the hammer and took aim at a nail which was still an inch out of the wood. The others laughed as he drew up his arm and gave a running commentary on his method. He paused for a while, holding the small crowd with his boasting.

'You see the grip? It's all in the grip. And of course excellent eye-to-hand co-ordination.'

'You're all talk. Watch him miss!'

The banter continued and then Max interrupted.

'Come on man. For God's sake hit the thing.'

The hammer came down and missed the nail by some inches. There was jeering and then another of the men took his turn.

The first three all missed the nail. Then Max took the hammer.

'Watch and learn. This is so simple my dogs could make a better job of it than you lot. Watch now.'

He swung the hammer down and missed. The group laughed

and Max swore. He took another go and missed again and then kept hammering.

'Hey cheat. Get the referee!'

'This won't count even if you do hit it.'

Max swore again and hammered until he had hit the nail flat into the wood.

'There. I told you – easy.'

He looked around at them and laughed so loudly that there was an echo from the mountain and the others' jeers turned to laugher as well.

'Go on Werner,' said one of them. 'Have a go.'

He did, though the audience was only half-watching now. They had started to talk amongst themselves, so even when he managed to hit the nail twice in succession there were only a few small cheers.

'Well done Werner. I think you win.'

'The nail's hardly gone in two millimetres,' said Max.

'But he hit it first time.'

'Yes, well, so he did. Come on, let's go inside and get more wine. That Anita will be missing me.'

They went back into the hut and as Max walked past Werner he shook him by the shoulders.

'Well done Werner. You hit the nail on the head there!'

Werner smiled and nodded as Max continued to grip him and stare into his eyes, his big red face up close.

'This is the life, eh Werner? Drinking and ski-ing and joking around with your friends?'

'Yes. It's a great day for it.'

'Friends. That's what it's about man. Life's nothing without your friends!'

Then Max slapped him several times on the back and they went into the hut. More wine was brought out and a plate of thick sweet cake for each man. They ate and drank until the sun had turned a deeper orange and was low on the blank horizon. Then it was time to go down. They fastened their boots and went outside to put on their skis. Again, Werner examined the faces of his companions. He looked for signs of anxiety, signs of dread. But their smiles were fixed and so was his and they pushed off down the valley, following Max.

It was three days since they had last been together, on the way to visit Clemenz. He wasn't a member of the group and not a friend of anyone. The best that could be said for Clemenz was that he had no friends. He had never held down any kind of proper job and seemed to have been stumbling around the town for years, since he was a child, causing trouble and getting in people's way. When the tourists came he was a liability, going into the bars and hotels, getting easily drunk and disgracing himself.

'You should see what it's like Werner,' one of the group had said on the way to the house. 'He's been losing me custom for years. Good custom too. There are people in this town who don't come to my restaurant because of some of the tricks he's pulled. Smashing into tables, pissing in the elevator. If you were me, you'd want to teach that little prick a lesson too.'

'And you know how he behaves with women,' said another.

Clemenz offended the older women and scared the young ones. His hands grabbed them in the supermarket or the post office and his leering face came up close in the street, making them shriek and then yell at him. However many beatings he had suffered at the hands of the husbands and fathers, there were never enough to make him stop.

'You know how he's always worrying my daughter. He was at it again last week. The little pervert.'

'And who has a wife who hasn't had trouble with him? He's a menace. And he'll bring us all into trouble some day. Drive away the tourists.'

Max orchestrated the complaints, as he always did. Nodding and encouraging and keeping things going, reminding them of old offences which they might have forgotten.

Werner understood, he told them he understood, but he knew that what they were planning was something more than teaching Clemenz a lesson. He felt no sympathy for the foolish boy, who had spoiled his evenings too, but he worried about taking him up on the mountain.

'Well he should be able to ski,' said Max. 'He's lived here all his life and he can't ski? It's not like he has no legs. What's his excuse? Apart from the lack of a brain?'

Then there had been laughter and everyone had joined in and Werner just couldn't tell who was sincere. So they went on to see Clemenz, who lived in a small house owned by his mother. The house was away from the road and they had to cross a broad icy field to reach it.

'Even his house is a bloody nuisance.'

'But you wouldn't want him living near human society would you? Better to have him out here with the animals. If only he could be kept here and not disturb us.'

They continued to abuse him and laugh together, confirming each other's opinions. By the time they approached the house, Clemenz had come out and stood on the balcony, grinning and looking nervous.

'Hey Clemenz,' shouted Max, waving.

'Hello.'

'Do you want to come ski-ing?'

Clemenz laughed a whining, high-pitched laugh.

'Ski-ing? No. No way.'

'What about drinking? Will you come drinking?'

'Yeah!' Clemenz smiled. He beamed and closed his eyes like a merry child. 'Drinking!'

'Come drinking with us.'

'Okay.'

'Then we'll go ski-ing,' said Max.

Clemenz just laughed and went inside to get his coat. Max turned to the others.

'See. He'll come ski-ing.'

The others looked at Max and no-one disagreed. There was silence until Clemenz appeared, wearing his normal scruffy clothes and an oversized anorak.

'I've got extra gear in the car,' said one of the men softly to the others. 'We'll get him properly equipped.'

Two hours later they were coming out of a cable car, half-way up the mountain. Clemenz, who was already drunk after being taken to two of the bars in town, was giggling, still nervous and happy.

'I don't know how. I've never really done it.'

'There's a lot of things you've never really done Clemenz,' said Max. 'Maybe if you do this, we'll let you do the other one. You know?' He winked. 'Find you a big girl.'

'A big girl! Yeah!' said Clemenz and he giggled wildly.

They fastened his boots and helped him clip on his skis. Then two of the men took an arm and guided him down twenty metres of the slope, very slowly, laughing and encouraging him as he went.

'This is good, isn't it Clemenz?'

'It's okay. It's not so bad as I thought.'

'You're doing alright. You've done some ski-ing before, haven't you?'

'When I was a boy, I did some. I went down slopes okay then.'

'So you can do it now.'

Clemenz got braver and went down a little by himself. They stayed by his side and helped him turn, but when he could go straight downhill he got up speed.

'Good, Clemenz, good!'

They led him further, stopping a few times for a swallow of brandy from a flask. After several kilometres of slow progress, they arrived at Anita's hut.

'Bravo, Clemenz. You deserve a drink.'

Wine, cold meats, games and shouting. Werner had drunk more than usual and had started to get a headache. He laughed along with the others and the laughter seemed louder than ever. He looked at Clemenz and hated his stupid face and his crazy innocence. The boy was drunk. Maybe he would puke and pass out, that would be the best thing for him. The boy. Werner didn't know how old he was, probably not so much younger than the rest of them, but he still seemed to be a boy. They ate bowls of stew and drank more wine, until the sun was down and the cable cars had stopped.

'Okay Anita,' said Max after the final game of hammering the nail, which Clemenz had been allowed to win. 'We're going. Goodbye, my sweetheart.'

'Will he be alright?' Said Anita.

'He can ski okay. He told us he's done quite a bit of ski-ing.

Anyway, we'll go carefully.'

They went out and helped Clemenz again with his skis. The snowfall was light but the wind had picked up. For the group of five, who knew the route from years of ski-ing, it was easy, but Clemenz was nervous even through his drunkenness.

'Wow. Oh, wow! Can't see much guys.'

His high laughter started off a slight echo down the valley. Hearing it, he laughed louder and then whooped, delighted with the retorts. The others laughed along and increased the pace.

'We're going fast now, guys.'

'You're doing good Clemenz. You've done more than you let on.'

'Well, when I was boy I did a lot. A lot of slopes.'

'I bet you did.'

'Come on Clemenz, let's get going properly. See if you can stay with us.'

'Wow!'

He shrieked and giggled and then Werner pretended not to hear anything. They continued their descent in single file, not looking back. The route was obvious enough until they had to get onto the last narrow path. At that point you could traverse the entire slope or go down it. Going down was steep and didn't lead to the bottom of the mountain. It would mean having to stop half-way down and walk through an area of trees to get back onto another piste. The group of five traversed and continued onto the narrow path. Werner put his head down. They were all ski-ing at normal pace now, making no allowances. There was no sound from anyone behind. Werner convinced himself that he had definitely heard no sound, no shrieking, no cry for help. When they reached the bottom they came together briefly.

'Okay,' said Max. 'Good ski-ing. Clemenz will follow on.'

There was a silence of less than a second while they swallowed the lie.

'He can give me back the gear some other time,' said the man who had lent it.

'Yeah.'

Then they dispersed, with quick goodbyes and no planning of

their next trip. Werner picked up his skis and walked to the road to take a bus back to his house. He had three more drinks when he got home and no dinner. Then he got into bed and pulled the blankets around him, screwing his eyes up tightly and breathing heavily. The next morning he wasn't sure whether he had actually slept at all.

* * *

Now, coming from Anita's hut again, following Max down the same slopes, Werner could hear the voice of Clemenz in his head. He had been hearing it for the last three days. The five men flowed down the mountain as if they were tied together, keeping to the long sweeping tracks of the man in front. Usually there would have been some fooling around at this point, someone would do a jump over a small ridge or turn and ski backwards for ten metres while the others shouted and raised their hands. But for the next five minutes they skied without interruption on the thick, well-packed snow, until the slope levelled off and Max stopped and looked around. The next stage of the route was the long traverse over to the narrow path. Max waited until they had all bunched behind him, then he nodded and set off slowly. The others followed him, looking to their right, down the mountain. Werner felt himself breathing more heavily now and his goggles had begun to steam over. He pulled them up to his forehead and continued to stare down the mountain.

They could have chosen to ski down, but that would have been too much of an admission of what they were doing here. Clemenz hadn't been missed in the town, not even by his mother who had taken nothing more than financial responsibility for him for many years. Werner had waited to hear news, for someone to say that the police had been called or at least the social services, but there had been nothing. So once they had crossed the slope, he felt something like relief, or at least a delay of the fearful moment. He watched the men in front of him straighten and stand taller, as if they were breathing more easily. Max turned.

'Going down right away?'

No-one answered for a while. Then one of the men said, 'No.'

The others looked at him. No-one usually disagreed with Max. But then they followed his gaze, which was not towards the leader but downwards. Werner went forward and now he could see a jacket, only ten metres or less down the slope. Snowfall had covered most of it, but the part that was still visible was recognisable. He was drawn to it and slowly skied down. He was wondering how close Clemenz had been behind them, managing to get most of the way across the slope and just failing at the end to make it onto the narrow path. Whose back had the boy been following before he lost momentum too early? And who did he make his final call to? Werner started to clear the snow off the jacket, ignoring Max who called out that it should be left alone and something about the police. Werner worked rapidly as the others gathered in a semi-circle behind him, silent now.

By the time he had uncovered the humped back and the crown of the head, there was really no need to dig anymore. But Werner knew that he had to keep going and felt calmer now, pulling his hood up not against the cold but to try to block out his sense of the four men behind. He kept his eyes on the body and ignored the mountains. It could have been just the two of them, him and Clemenz, on a small patch of ground at the most private of burial ceremonies. Then there wouldn't need to be all the trouble of getting the body down into town, with people coming out to see the stretcher and rumours rebounding around the houses so fast that by the time he got home there would be visitors coming to ask him what he knew. And it seemed cruel to haul Clemenz through the cold again, after all that he had suffered.

Werner stood up and took hold of the frozen corpse.

'No, Werner. Leave it.'

But he lifted the body from the snow and turned it over before he could be stopped. For such a light man, such a boy, Clemenz had grown heavy. His face was set in a grimace, the face of a man who was in pain from freezing and who was only half-fighting against death. Werner stared at it, not yet horrified but knowing that the horror would come and would stay with him.

'Christ. Where did he think he was going?'

'He must have turned too early.'

They continued for a while with their absurd, pretend conjectures and Werner wanted to tell them to stop, but he was tired again. He looked around the group and still there was nothing revealed. Finally a phone call was made and snow-sleds came roaring up the valley. Werner looked into the darkening sky; Clemenz wasn't even worth a helicopter. He watched the body being packaged up and tied to one of the sleds. The group was to follow the police down for interviews at the station. Max was looking around, trying to hold each man's eye. Some men gave him a curt nod and Werner watched them do so. He took account of who was determined and who had to look away.

He turned from Max. The laughter, the big face, the back-slapping and the forced brotherhood didn't bother him now. He could feel the tiredness and the cold in his bones and wondered how many nights it would be before he was able to think of something other than the mountain. They skied down in formation, so slowly that Werner could occasionally close his eyes against the glare of the snow and try to find comfort in a few seconds of darkness.

Show And Tell

Simon Armitage

Marlon said, 'That was the school on the phone.
They want me to go in and talk to Jennifer's class.'
'You? Why you? You don't know shit about shit,'
said his significant other.
'All the other dads have done it. They say it's my turn.'
'Well, you'd better not make a pig's arse of it,
for your precious little Jenny's sake. But don't ask me,
I'm only the wicked step-mother,' she said.
Then she went back to her on-line taxidermy lesson.

For the next week or so Marlon was in a muck-sweat,
fretting about the talk he'd agreed to give.
Finally he decided a little show and tell session wouldn't hurt.
Something to focus their attention – concentrate their minds.
The morning duly arrived, and although Marlon had visited the school
on several occasions, today the route seemed unfamiliar
and through a part of town far rougher than he remembered.
After bottoming the car on a truly formidable sleeping policeman
he pulled up at a barrier. A man in a serge-blue uniform
spoke to him from behind the metal grille of a fortified kiosk.
'I.D.' he said.
Marlon scrambled for his driving licence in the glove compartment.
'I've come to talk to Class 9.'
'Sign this disclaimer,' said the guard,
then pointed to the reception entrance without removing his gauntlet.
As instructed, Marlon parked up, passed through a metal-detector
then followed a line of dried blood splashes
to a room at the end of a basement corridor.
Halfway along Jennifer spotted her father, took one look at him –
especially at his shoes – and bolted.
Inside the classroom about twenty young teenagers

were sprawled across tables and chairs, scratching and yawning.
Thinking that surprise was his best tactic,
Marlon gulped down a big breath of air,
pulled a small rust-coloured stone out of his pocket
and said, 'Has anyone here ever seen a shooting star?
Has anyone ever held a piece of outer-space in their hand?
Does anyone know what this is?'
A boy at the back in a khaki body-warmer put his hand up.
'What's your ride, man?'
'Excuse me?' said Marlon.
'What kind of car do you drive, granddad?' said the boy.
'A Clio,' Marlon told him.
'That's a pussy's car,' said the boy, and the whole class sniggered.
Marlon was still holding the space-rock
between his thumb and index finger, but awkwardly,
like a robot picking up an egg. Another boy
with a swastika tattoo on his earlobe strolled right up to Marlon
and said, 'Have you got any money, or no?'
'Not on me,' lied Marlon.
'Come on, we're wasting our time with this muppet,'
said the young Nazi.
With their hands rammed in their pockets
the rest of the class followed him out of the room.
Only a small, bespectacled girl remained in her seat.
She was very small indeed – just a tiny dot of a thing.
In a voice like the squeaking wheel of a pram she said,
'That's no meteorite. It's just a pebble you picked up on the road.
Isn't it, mister? Isn't it?'
Marlon said, 'Do you know my daughter, Jennifer?'
'You're not Jenny's dad. Jenny's dad's got no legs,' she squeaked.
Marlon wasn't crying exactly, but behind his eyes
tears were streaming like rain down the windows of an all-night café.
'Look, I'll show you the way to the caretaker's office
then you'll have to make a run for it,' said the girl.
'But it'll have to look like there's been a struggle.
A black eye at least, and maybe a broken nose, just to be safe.'
Marlon thought about the porcelain cheekbones
beneath the pale skin of her face.

'I could never hit a child,' he said.
'Stupid – it's me whacking you,' she said,
pulling a telescopic truncheon out of her book bag.
Marlon turned away from the blow. Just then Jennifer's face appeared in the panel of safety glass in the classroom door. Suddenly the meteorite started to glow.

Snappy

Paul Duncan

My name is George and I am five and I am scared. I am locked in the bathroom with my arms wrapped around the toilet and my eyes closed and tears coming down my cheeks and I am scared because Snappy is outside he wants to come in to play with me but I do not want to play with him, he is big and I am small.

I have my arms wrapped around the toilet because there is no bath in this bathroom. The bath is next door in the other bathroom. The room I am in is also called the bathroom even though there is no bath in it I do not know why. This room should be called the toilet room but it is not. It is called the bathroom. Dad called it the Crap Factory once in front of me and laughed but Mum said 'no, that room is called the bathroom, don't put ideas in his head, and anyway we should not be talking about the bathroom in the dining room, it is not right.' We should only talk about the bathroom when we are in the bathroom I suppose so that is why I am talking about the bathroom now because I am in the bathroom hiding from Snappy.

Snappy is outside making happy noises. Deep in his throat Snappy makes happy noises and bangs on the door and wants to come in and play with me. The door bangs and shakes and shivers and splits and Snappy jumps against the door and wants to come in. Snappy is a bad boy he made a mess downstairs and I will get blamed for the mess because Snappy is mine and I get the blame for everything around here it is not fair. I am glad I locked the door. I do not want to play with Snappy. I am scared of Snappy he is a bad boy he gets me into trouble. I shout at the door and shout, 'Go away Snappy you are a bad boy go away' but he does not go away he only bangs on the door harder and makes more happy noises.

I am scared of Snappy.

First I will tell you about why I am scared of Snappy. No first I will tell you about how me and Snappy met, about how me and Snappy became friends. It is a good story. No first I will tell you about the old man in the woods, it is sort of the same story as how I met Snappy but it is the beginning and Mum says 'always begin at the beginning' so I better start with the old man in the woods because that is the beginning so I will start there. No... the real start of the story is the Bad Misters that is right. The Bad Misters is the real beginning. So I will start there.

First I will tell you about the Bad Misters.

The Bad Misters are horrible old men who want to take children away and do stuff to them that is not nice. My Mum told me about them and my Dad told me about them. They pull up in cars when you are walking to the shops and try to take you away and do stuff. They are like witches but they look like old men and they smell funny and they live in caves. They hang around outside the school gates and say they have some puppies at home and do you want to go home with them and see the puppies but they do not have puppies really. Or. Or if they do have puppies then they eat them in front of you and make you eat the puppies as well. In the cave where they live they keep lots of puppies in cages and when they bring somebody home with them they put them in a cage and then eat the puppies in front of them to scare them. Then they make you eat the puppies and then they take you out of the cage and do stuff to you. They hang around in parks too. If you saw a Bad Mister in a park and you were on your own he would try to grab you and do stuff to you. Like. Like if you kicked your ball near him he would take your ball and eat it and not give it back. Or. Or if a Bad Mister got hold of you in the park he would take you somewhere dark and make you sniff glue with him. Like. Like he would make you sniff glue with him and then he would make you hunt puppies with him and hang around the school gates with him. Mum told me if I saw a Bad Mister and he asked me about puppies I should run away quick and tell a Grown Up. But Bad Misters are Grown Ups too so I do not know what she meant. I will ask her she is downstairs. She is in a mess downstairs.

Snappy is outside. He wants to come in.

So I knew not to talk to Bad Misters but one day I was in the park with Dad and Dad was talking to Auntie Julie and they were both smoking tabs. Even though Mum does not want Dad smoking tabs because it is not good for him but Dad always smokes tabs when we go to the park and he always talks to Auntie Julie. Dad laughs and says that when he smokes tabs 'it is a secret, it is our little secret,' he says, and gives me a pound, and says, 'shush, this is our little secret and don't tell your Mam about Auntie Julie either, they don't get along.' It is our little secret Dad says, and then he gives me another pound.

So I was in the park with Dad and Aunt Julie and I was kicking my ball and I kicked my ball too hard and my ball shot into the woods at the side of the park. There are woods at the side of the park but I am not allowed in them they are scary. I am not allowed in to the woods because... because Bigger Boys hang around in there and sniff glue with girls so I am not allowed in. Dad calls the woods the Unwanted Pregnancy Woods but I do not know what he means. I asked him what he means once and he looked sad and ruffled my hair and said, 'You'll find out soon enough. Just you stay out of the Forest of Big Mistakes for as long as you can, and you'll live a happy life.' So I remembered what Dad had said when I kicked my ball into the woods.

I shouted my Dad that I had lost my ball and could he come and get it for me. But Dad was busy smoking tabs and talking to Aunt Julie with his back to me and he only waved at me from behind his head not looking so I went into the woods on my own.

I know it was naughty but I wanted my ball I did not want a Bad Mister to eat my ball so I went in.

I ran into the woods quick because I did not want to stay in the woods for long because the woods are scary. Not scary like a picture of a witch in a book is scary but scary like the first day of school is scary. Like scary like a trip to the dentist is scary. Tingles in the tummy scary. So I ran into the woods quickly and looked for my ball my ball was bright red it was easy to see it was near a big pile of leaves. But then the leaves began to move and shake and it was not a big pile of leaves it was a big pile of man sleeping under some leaves. The man sat up and the leaves fell away and the man was looking right at me and the man was smiling. Smiling right at me and the man was saying 'is this your ball, son?' and the man picked up the ball and held it in his hand. And I got scared because this man was a Bad Mister because he smelled funny and he would eat my ball and he would take me away to see some puppies and he would make me eat some puppies and I did not want to eat some puppies because puppies are nice. But. But he did not look like a Bad Mister he looked nice. He had a big white beard like Father Christmas and he was smiling and he looked like Granddads look on telly. He did not look like my real Granddad. My real Granddad is small and yellow and lies very still in his bed he is boring. This telly Granddad in the woods looked plump and happy and his cheeks were red like my ball and his beard was long and white and bushy. He waved me over and said, 'Don't be afraid, come over here and say hello. Come and get your ball,'

I went over because I was not afraid and I wanted my ball. He looked nice he was nice.

He patted the ground next to him and I sat down. He held my ball up to his face and said, 'That is a nice ball but I have something better than a nice ball. Would you like to see it?'

He put his arm around me and pulled me in close to him so I could smell his breath it was bad. He fiddled around in his trousers for a bit and then said, 'This is a very special item and I don't show it to just anyone. This is a secret. This is our little secret. Would you like me to show it to you?'

I knew all about our little secrets like Dad and the tabs so I said yes. The happy old man looked very happy when I said this. Then he showed me his little secret. He pulled it out of his pocket and held it up to my face. It was an egg. It was an egg bigger than a scrambled egg but smaller than an Ostrich egg like on telly. It was a different colour to a normal egg it was all browny and red. He put it in my hand and it was all warm and glowy. It felt nice in my hand. Then he said, 'isn't that the nicest egg you've ever seen? Wouldn't you like to take that egg home with you to love and take care of and then, in a little while, see what hatches forth into the world?' I said I would and then he said, 'it's yours, son but remember it's a secret, don't tell your

Mam and Dad about it or they'll take it from you and put it in the bin. Keep it warm and keep it under your bed until it's hatched, and then you'll have a new friend to play with.'

I thanked the man and I got up and started to walk away. Then I stopped and turned around and asked him what my new friend's name was.

'Name?' The old man started laughing he laughed a long time and then he said, 'Call him Snappy.'

That is how Snappy and me became friends. I ran out of the woods and ran over to my Dad and Auntie Julie. Dad shouted at me because I had lost my ball and we went home. I did not tell him about Snappy. I hid the egg in the back of my trousers and walked home very carefully. Oh yeah I forgot to get my ball back off the old man. He must still have it now. We did a swap without me knowing. I wish I still had my ball instead of Snappy. I wish I could swap back.

* * *

The door shakes and shakes and shakes. The bolt on the bathroom door is all broken and twisted. Snappy is outside I can see parts of him through the edges of the door that have broken away he is coming inside to see me. I can see his eye looking at me his mouth smiling at me he is happy. He is coming inside to see me.

* * *

I put Snappy under my bed like the man said to. Snappy looked silly under my bed all alone so I took an empty box from downstairs and put Snappy in the empty box. But. But Snappy still looked silly and sad and lonely in that big empty box on his own so I took a jumper a Christmas Jumper I did not like and put that in the bottom of the box and put Snappy on top and wrapped the jumper around Snappy around the egg and that looked better. I did not know what else to do. I got some crisps from downstairs and poured them into the box in case the egg got hungry. Then I did not know what else to do but I remembered Snappy was a secret so I closed up the flaps of the box and I pushed Snappy all the way under my bed with the dust and the hairs and forgot about Snappy. I forgot about Snappy and I went out to play.

I forgot about Snappy for I do not know how long, a long time. I forgot about Snappy until one night late at night I heard sounds bumping sounds from under my bed. At first I was scared because a Bad Mister had got under my bed and was banging on the bottom of my bed looking for me. Then I remembered Snappy and got happy because Snappy was born, Snappy was under my bed, Snappy was my new friend. I jumped out of my bed and fished out the box and opened the flaps. Oh. Snappy was born and he did not look like a puppy he did not look like a kitten he did not look like a chicken. He looked... he looked like a lizard like a crocodile like a dinosaur. He was all red coloured and stood on two hind legs and had two little dangling arms and a little tail and a funny oblong head full of teeth. He looked up at me and he smiled and he had lots and lots of teeth in that smile. He had eaten all the crisps and most of the Christmas Jumper too. He was hungry, he was a hungry Snappy. He tried to jump up and get out of the box but he was too little. He was like me he was too little. The bumping noises were the sounds of Snappy jumping up at the sides of the box trying to get out but he could not get out because he was too little. He looked up at me and smiled and snapped his head together twice SNAP SNAP. That is why he is called Snappy he likes to SNAP SNAP.

I crept downstairs because it was late and I did not want to wake up Mum or Dad. I went to the fridge and took out some chicken left over from Sunday lunch it was Sunday. I crept back upstairs and went over to the box and dropped the chicken in for Snappy. Snappy looked happy and scoffed the chicken down quicksmarts SNAP SNAP. He looked up at me and then jumped up he wanted to come out. He could not come out it was a school night I was sleepy. I told Snappy goodnight and closed up the box and pushed it under the bed and went back to bed I was sleepy. I slept until morning until Mum got me up and I went downstairs and had my breakfast and Mum took me to school I forgot about Snappy. I forgot about Snappy until I got home from school and watched telly and went on the computer and had my tea and went to my room to do homework. I forgot about Snappy until I heard those bumping noises again only louder this time. Then I remembered Snappy he must be hungry.

I pulled out the cardboard box. But. But it had all holes in it. Snappy had put holes in it trying to get out. I lifted back the flaps to look at Snappy. But. But Snappy was bigger now he had grown up. He was as big as a puppy no he was bigger he was as big as a dog. I went to pet him like a dog but he snapped at my hand SNAP SNAP. His box was too small for him now. He jumped and nearly got out but I pulled down the flaps to stop him. The box shakes and he tries to get out. I cannot let him get out or Mum will see him she will go mad she will throw Snappy in the bin.

I thought for ages about what to do then I remembered my old toy box in the closet it was full of toys I did not want anymore. It was big and made of wood and it had a lid with a lock and a key it would keep Snappy inside keep him safe from Mum. I took out the toybox and undid the lock with the key and poured out the toys on the floor. I picked up the cardboard box with Snappy inside it shakes about in my arms he wants to come out. I emptied Snappy into the toybox. He was at the bottom of the toybox he looked smaller again now. He jumped up but he cannot get out now he looked smaller. He looked sad his toothy head looked sad. He made sad noises in his throat, he looked sad. I went to pet Snappy's head but Snappy tried to bite me again SNAP SNAP. He is a bad boy he is naughty. I closed the lid on Snappy and locked the lock and put the key in my pocket and pushed Snappy into the closet and closed the door. No food for you Snappy you are a bad boy. The closet door was thick and I could not hear Snappy anymore. I did my homework and forgot about Snappy. I went to bed and forgot about Snappy. I went to school and forgot about Snappy.

I forgot about Snappy until I came home from school with Mum. Dad was waiting for us in the livingroom he looked cross. He looked cross and the toybox was at his feet. The toybox was shaking at his feet. Snappy was still inside the toybox and he wanted to come out. The lid is still locked but the toybox shakes because Snappy wants to come out.

'What is the meaning of this?' says my Dad.

I say it is Snappy he is hungry he wants to come out, it is a surprise.

'What is that thing, Tom?' says my Mum, I am in trouble.

'I don't know. I went into soft lad's room because I could hear all this racket coming from the closet. I open the door and, surprise surprise, our George has a visitor.'

Mum looked cross with me she walks over to stand with Dad. 'What is it? What is it? A dog?'

Dad says, 'I don't know what it is, I can't find the key so I brought it down here to ask George.'

And I say it is not a dog it is Snappy he is... he is like a dinosaur he wants to come out.

'I can see he wants to come out. Poor thing is probably starving. I thought we taught you better than this, George. Now, where is the key?'

Oh yeah the key I forgot about the key it is still in my pocket. I give Dad the key and walk away quickly he is mad at me he might give me the slipper. He and Mum looked cross they bent down they opened the lock they threw back the lid they let Snappy out.

Oh.

Oh Snappy has grown bigger much bigger. He jumps out the box like a crackerjack. He jumps onto Dad. He jumps onto Mum. Snappy makes a mess. Snappy makes a big mess. I get scared and run away and Snappy follows me he follows me to the bathroom I lock the door I am scared Snappy is outside he wants to come in and play with me.

The bathroom door breaks in and down and comes apart. Snappy is there in front of me. He is happy he is making happy noises.

Oh my Snappy what big teeth you have.

Dad

Andrew McMillan

i)
each Wednesday marked
by the arrival of your scarf
slung round ironic,
except it's cold outside and so
it's just a scarf,
your arms just arms
except they're piled high
with books as if the rubble
of a frantic library
has descended into them

ii)
when,
on catching me topless
with Thom Gunn and grinning,
you nodded as if to say that you
were proud and dad that's why
I am too

iii)
you tell me that you
met Thom Gunn
and all I think
is that I want the
hand he grasped in
his. I want to chop it
off and, dad, I want
to frame it by my bed

and dream of boys
who maim their fathers
for their hands
and frame them
by their beds
cos once those fathers
grasped my hand
in theirs.

Don't Step On The Cracks

John Glander

The crocodiles got him. I knew that it was going to happen. I told him that if he stepped on the cracks between the paving stones, one day they would rise up and drag him down. He laughed at me and went walking where his feet fell.

'Come on Tony, are you stupid? We gave up believing in that rubbish years ago.'

The logical part of me knew that he was right, it had been a childish game and we should have long since put it behind us. That wasn't the point. I knew that it could happen and the crocodiles didn't have to be mystical green creatures that came up out of the ground.

'You don't know that it isn't true.'

He laughed again.

'You're so bloody thick.'

He told everyone that I had a pea sized brain. It wasn't just for talking about the dangers hidden in the cracks. I knew that I was a bit slower on the uptake than a lot of people, but that didn't make me stupid the way that Ryan claimed. For a best friend, he could be pretty nasty.

'You shouldn't let him treat you that way,' Katie told me. 'It's not fair.'

I just shrugged. 'He always has.' You sort of get used to things after a while.

'That doesn't make it right,' she said. 'I know what you mean about the cracks.'

'You step on them,' I pointed out.

'I'm immune,' she told me, 'as long as I put my left shoe on first.'

I liked Katie. We seemed to speak the same language and I could talk to her because she was going out with my best mate.

Katie was beautiful. She had blonde hair and blue eyes and amazing curves which had started to show when she was at junior school so by the time she was fifteen, she was amazing. All the boys wanted her. Ryan was the one who had her at the time, only I didn't think he treated her very well.

It was the night that she dumped him that the crocodiles got him. As he walked away, I yelled something after him. I could never remember what I said, but I knew what he yelled back.

'Grow up you wussy.'

He only got about half way along the High Street before they got him. I know he was my best friend, but I would say that he deserved it for what he had done.

The hospital did pretty well with the repairs, but Katie's nose was a bit odd from then on, there was a twist to her mouth so her words were slightly slewed, and she could never see properly out of her left eye again.

There was a lot of fuss when Ryan couldn't be found the next day. Of course I didn't tell anyone what had happened, at least not with the crocodiles. They knew what he had done to Katie, but no-one believed the reason. They all had their own idea. A girl like her with boobs that big had to be putting it out for everyone.

'I wasn't a virgin,' she told me many years later, a fact that I already knew. 'I lost it before I knew what it was, and then for about six months I thought that was what I had to do. It didn't take long to work out I was wrong. I didn't put it around the way they said.'

'I know,' I said, kissing her swollen middle. 'I was slow, not stupid.'

'You were stupid,' she said. 'You were stupid the way I was, letting Ryan fool you for so long and doing everything that he told you to do.'

'I didn't shag him,' I said, though there had been talk to the effect it was what I wanted.

'I didn't either,' she said. 'That was the problem.'

'I know.' I could only kiss her. 'It's all in the past Katie, you don't have to worry.' I knew why she was having strange thoughts, we had been warned.

She ran her fingers through my hair. 'If he'd told you to do it, would you have shagged me?'

'It never happened.' I knew that wasn't what she was asking me. 'It only happened once, the first time with Martha Stone and she was up for it. I don't think you would have been.' I didn't think that at the age I had been then, I would have been able to, she would have so over-excited me.

'I always wanted to,' she said. 'I thought it was something about me which was stopping you. I never thought you were gay, that was a stupid idea.'

'Let's not worry about what didn't happen,' I said. 'Let's stick with what did happen.'

It might not have happened. After that night there was more trouble than any of us had ever known. Katie had needed to go to the hospital and her parents were furious with just about everyone, me included. Ryan was nowhere to be found. The crocodiles had got him. There was no coming back from them.

* * *

Seven years was a long time. I had been walking along the High Street, when a voice said, 'Don't step on the cracks, you never know what could happen.'

'Did you put on your left shoe first?'

'I always do.'

She looked amazing despite the imperfections. I hadn't thought what would happen if we were to meet again. I assumed that such a lovely girl would be married, probably with a couple of kids, but I was wrong.

'Who would want lop-sided Katie?'

There was a new cafe on the north side of Draper Street with continental style street tables. Some people looked uncomfortable when we sat there.

'I sound stupid to match being a bit slow.'

'I don't believe it,' I told her. 'I would say thoughtful.'

'You were always sweet.' She tilted up her head to blow smoke at the sky. 'No-one ever saw me the way that you did. We can be so stupid at times.'

'It's those periods in our lives that matter,' I reminded her. 'Some of us just need more time to sort ourselves out.'

'You look as though you've done it.'

We had a lot to catch up on and that was the original excuse for meeting again. We still felt that we needed excuses, not that it lasted long. Three months later we were lovers.

'Why did we never do this before?' she asked.

'You know why.' I didn't want to go over the past. 'It was worth waiting.'

'Oh my god yes.' She clung to me.

'I still can't believe you're on your own and don't say you were waiting.'

She laughed. 'Oh I was, I was waiting for the right moment and when I saw you on the High Street and still avoiding the cracks in the pavement, I knew the moment had come.'

'It's habit,' I told her. 'The whole crocodile thing was never real.' There was a part of me that wouldn't let go in case something bad happened, though it was only on the High Street I made a point of doing it.

'Will you tell our children about the crocodiles?'

Two hours before we had only kissed and she was talking about children. It was possible. She had insisted that we be natural, that it had to be real or it would be meaningless and I knew what she meant. In point of fact we were married before she was pregnant. We decided that day we were going to get married.

'I can't believe that you weren't snapped up long ago.'

She laughed. 'With my twist, the fact that girls have to be stick thin and my boobs are far too big so most people think they're fake, and I smoke rather than snort.'

The world was indeed a strange place. The one where crocodiles lurked under the paving stones ready to snap up the unwary was much easier to understand.

* * *

Susan never believed in the crocodiles.

'Don't be silly daddy, there are no crocodiles.'

'Why not?'

She was a curiously serious little girl, with my looks rather than those of her mother which was probably a good thing. Katie had not had an easy life because of her looks.

'They need water to live in,' she said.

'There's water down there,' I pointed out.

'In pipes and they wouldn't be able to get out of the pipes.'

She knew because it was a period when exotic pets were turning up in drains and the dear little croc babies soon got to be a pain and more than one was flushed into the sewer. Susan was being literal. She had no hint of the mystical in her. A lot of people were later to call her hard-nosed, but they didn't know her. It wasn't the crocodiles that got her, they would have stood no chance. I was never sure what it was, it shouldn't have happened to such a lovely person, but then it was always the nicest people who suffered. Susan was and is a sweet person but for anyone to find that out they have to make an effort to get under that hard crust and these days few will bother.

* * *

One morning Katie put her shoes on the wrong way around. She couldn't find the left shoe and we had to get going so she put on the one she had while I crawled around looking for the other. It didn't matter, it really didn't matter, but she felt it. That was the morning we found out.

The fact that the left side of her face wasn't quite right was down to what had happened the night the crocodiles got Ryan. There had been nerve damage. What had not been spotted at the time, probably because it had been masked and was tiny, was deeper damage. When Katie started to slur her words more and was having trouble with her co-ordination, I insisted she be checked out. When they did the scan, they found the mass. It would have been there whatever shoe she put on first. It had become critical to the point where they couldn't operate on her. They offered chemo, but I think that she knew that at best it would only keep her going a short time and she didn't want to go through the pain. She didn't want the people she loved to remember her as a twisted bald old woman, not that she was old.

'Don't cry for me,' she said. 'I got lucky. We've had a good time together, I have good children and grandchildren, even at my age.' Susan had been rather quick off the mark. 'You make sure you look after yourself.'

I wasn't sure, but I suppose it was the crocodiles who got her in the end.

Mandy told me about them. I don't know where she heard the tale, it wasn't from Susan and I hadn't said anything.

'What about in Draper Street?' I asked. 'They're so close together you would have to walk on tip-toe.'

The council had fallen prey to the fashion of laying bricks rather than slabs and while the pattern was good, I knew they wouldn't last and they were so slippery when wet.

'That's different, grandad,' Mandy said, looking up at me with big eyes full of Katie. 'They would have to be tiny ones and they couldn't really hurt you.'

It was a sophisticated idea for one so young.

'I don't know how she works it out,' Susan confessed. 'I said nothing.'

'Don't look at me,' I told her. 'That's something which belongs to a time long ago, if not far away.'

'When everything was brighter and better,' she said.

I had to laugh. 'Stupid idea, it never was, though I don't think there was so much fear being generated back then.'

'You and mum...' She began.

'Not then. It was her and my best friend until he turned on her and killed her.'

It had taken more than thirty years but it had been his fists that night which had killed her. He had put his hand up her skirt once too often but when she told him that it was over, then he had hit her and tried to have her anyway.

'There's nothing you can do,' she said, 'And you did get me.'

The way she said it made me laugh.

'The ice maiden with a daughter.'

'The best way to be,' she said. 'I thought that he was for real daddy or I wouldn't have let him that close.'

'Life is risk,' I reminded her, 'And the strangest events can work out for you in the end.'

* * *

The council decided to re-lay the High Street. To be fair, the slabs were cracking and it was getting dangerous. Mandy was sad.

'The crocodiles will have to go and live somewhere else,' she said.

'They've probably been here too long,' I told her. 'Time for them to go and have fun. It's the turn of the bears to come in to chase naughty little girls who don't clean their teeth.'

'I am not naughty and bears are too fat to live in cracks.'

She had to stop where the men were working just to see what was under the slabs. It was dark earth with a layer of sand that had merged with it over the years and they were as hard as concrete. The men had to resort to using drills to break it up so it could be levelled and new sand put down.

'I can see a crocodile tail,' Mandy said. 'It's white because they live in the dark.'

It wasn't a crocodile tail. It was a human bone, a complete set of human bones.

Lost And Found

Kelly Stanger

I've lost my mind.
I must have left her in the pub last night.
She was last seen I think
necking shots of black vodka over ice.

The night is blurry, I'd had a few myself,
but fragments of a heated spat
are pushing slowly through the haze.

She got chatty with the barman,
laughing and touching his arm
and when I called her a whore
she slapped my face,
grabbed her smokes and went outside.

When I followed her to the beer garden
her face creased into that scowl
I've come to despise
then she wrote I love you on a rizla,
rolled it with tobacco and lit it with a fuck-you smile
blowing curls of smoke into my eyes.

What does that mean, I screamed
as she staggered back inside
and ordered another black vodka over ice.

I Think My Muse Is Having An Affair

Kelly Stanger

It started as a whisper late at night
he brought me diamonds wrapped in his tongue
unfurled them in the shadows
breathed rose scent
and velvet petals through my hair,
dissolved me with his liquid tones,
said I was his only one.

Then he started coming late,
bringing clutches of dandelions
from the side of the road,
daisies rived from their roots
hanging their heads in petrol-fume shame.
Then came the unfurling of malt whisky slurs in my ear,
the lipstick scented kisses and whispers of I love you
thin as water through my hair
as I turned away.

These days he comes at all hours,
garbles in Ancient Greek
so I can't understand.
He brings his lovers and they stomp in a circle
chanting rhythms that swell and conflate,
banging bugarabu drums and shaking rainsticks.
I hide under the sheets
cover my ears, but he knows I am here.

Tits Like Elephants' Ears

Natalya Lowndes

When he got drunk he always asked the same question. It had become a ritual and the pitch of his voice deepened.

'Do you know, Shelagh,' he boomed, hamming like an Edwardian actor, 'Do you know how I was educated?'

She was his favourite model, kept her poses, never whined. At this stage he was always working at full stretch, greedy for her, laying her open. She never saw the paint go on, only the brush jerking and slithering.

'Christ,' she once said to a girlfriend, 'Half an hour with him and I'm itching for it.'

'No, Edwin, my dear old sod, I do not know how you were educated.'

She was expected to say this. It was an extra bit tacked on to the modelling, like talking dirty. She'd learned to do it with verve and came to every Life Class with a little bit of what he fancied in the talking way.

'Not up against a brick wall round the back of a Rotherhithe boozer when you was thirteen, eh Edwin, my duck?'

He chuckled. 'Have another, dear, help yourself.'

They were drinking Muscadet. It disagreed with her at this time of the month. He knew it did.

'My question, Shelagh?'

'Stop poncing me about, Edwin.'

'How was I educated?'

'On summer clouding, Edwin.'

'On summer clouding, Shelagh, summer clouding. Have a decent drink, dear. There's some Gordons in the bag.'

Shelagh eased herself up, naked except for her fur-lined ankle boots.

'God, I'm ugly', she said. 'I'm a fucking walking liability. I got tits like an elephants' ears. And there's my belly...'

A rainbow iridescence flickered along the oily palette knife. He set about the canvas with patrician bravura.

Shelagh drank the gin neat from a cup.

'Edwin,' she said, suddenly morose, 'Do you think anyone'll ever, ever *interfere* with me again?'

He ignored her.

'She-she.' It was a soft moan. 'Did I ever tell you about the time my Dad's foreman fell through the roof at Vickers Armstrong?'

And he remembered the North Circular Road in the 1960s where, every May and June, his father and a bunch of convicts on day release, whitewashed roof lights of aircraft assembly hangars.

'Do you know what Summer Clouding is, Shelagh?'

'Fuck it, Eddy, you know it's a game, you never told me...'

'Guess.' Now he was at the peremptory stage.

Over soon, she told herself, and then we'll get the sister thing.

'Cockless shagging, angels do it,' she said wearily, aching from the posture he had devised for her, the onset of her menses, and the truth of her naked body. 'Like that Mills and Boon stuff...'

'Like Barbie dolls between the legs?'

'Darning-eggs, wee-wee no fuckee fuckee...'

One last slash at the picture plane angled up and out beyond the perspective. Quiet, then:

'Do you know, Shelagh, my green-grass Irish slut..?'

Wearily. 'Yes, Edwin, yes, you cock gasbag, you know I don't know and I don't give a donkey's wag what the fuck you want me to say because I'm tired and unfuckable and swag-bellied like a black Council shite-bag and nobody's coming up me again forever and ever and ever, and I'm sad, Eddie...'

'Edwin,' he said.

'I'm sad, Edwin.'

'Sad, She-she?'

'Sad.'

'I'm sad, too, She-she.'

It always ended like this with her drunk, him very drunk.

'I saw my sister the other day,' he murmured, suddenly changing tack, illogical and self-absorbed. 'The colour of fish.'

Sheilagh went rigid. 'Oh, Christ, Ed, Christ, not that today, not the sister-thing. I get so as I can't sleep from it, it's like drowning, it's like being eaten in bits...'

* * *

As a small boy he believed the death of his sister had exempted him from death. Later on, he understood the absurdity of this belief, but it had remained with him as an article of faith. Consequently, he had made no pact with himself to reject speculation about the future. On the contrary, he rejoiced in a world of infinite possibilities.

At first, admirers of his work found it too hard to disguise their revulsion at this queer line of sister chat. To them it was a gestural palaver he needed to get himself going. Like Shelagh, they had grown to sense when it was coming on. Unlike her, they could run. She bore the brunt. She had to, she needed the money. Well, that wasn't the whole story with Shelagh, but almost all.

Occasionally she took an interest.

'What was she like?'

'When?'

Up to then he'd been very peaceable, she thought. That mood came on him sometimes like the serene postlude to a fit. She wanted to take advantage.

'When she was, you know, any time like when she was.'

'Here, you mean?'

She looked round the deserted studio as if from the summit of a rock. 'Yeah, I suppose,' she said, a slight catch in her voice. 'Anywhere.'

He was priming a six by four canvas, absorbed. 'I don't remember except for the last time. It's always like that, it's only the last time that counts.'

'Ah,' she said. 'Only the last time. Well, what was she like that last time?'

'Do you know the Barents Sea, She-Sha?' He called her that

often. It was like having her temples douched in cologne. She trembled ever so slightly, all over.

'Not a pub, is it?'

'The Barents Sea is very cold, and very deep. Things lie in the dark forever at the bottom of the Barents Sea, wouldn't you say, She-Sha?'

'I expect so, Edwin, if you say so.'

Bugger it. Just her luck to have got caught out, sticking her nose in. The flesh on her thighs stiffened under a coarse, red rash. Bugger it.

He was rinsing off the primer from his hands with a yellow polystyrene sponge.

'She comes from there,' he said declaratively, as if there were an argument to be brooked.

'From where?'

'From the bottom.'

Shelagh made a quick calculation. His mood switches were directly related to intake. How much had he had? A few at the Queen of Prussia, a lot here since. She satisfied herself by the formula she had devised a long time ago. Ten to one, twelve to one. He was all right, just a bit gone. Dreamy.

She was quite wrong. He took a canvas-backed chair and sat opposite her, their knees touching.

'You know what I see?' he said.

Of course, she didn't, she couldn't, she wouldn't if she could, so she said, 'Yes.'

He ignored her. 'She had a lovely figure, slender, big-breasted.'

'Yes, Edwin.'

'And do you know how I see her? I see her at rest, the geometry of her limbs relaxed, in a huddle, and tiny fish with goggle-mouths are feeding off her pores. She shines in the black, and she turns, Shelagh, she turns, and in the whole of that great, freezing sea she is the only thing that makes any sound...'

He saw his sister rising on the warm up-welling of an abyssal fount as translucent as the skin of a saint, hung round with thousands of incorruptible bells that purled the water to a fluff, the brine on her luminescent, the thousands of bells the size of an infant's little fingernail, swaying in the equinoctial midnight.

He hadn't always been like this.

Sheilagh remembered that day in the garden where foliage erupted from every corner. The borders and shrubberies filled with a flood of new growth and when she took an audible gasp, clenched her mouth tight, her shirt came away and his free hand moved in spasm, gently twisting one nipple between finger and thumb. He had gripped the tight curls at the nape of her neck pressing her towards him and she remembered the way her long black skirt had been thrown up over her naked back, and his hand fasted between her thighs. The lower part of her body had twisted to and fro and she had wanted to grunt like an animal.

She sat still, shutting one eye and then the other, dreaming of his mouth and hands and eyes and when her tits had been full and Ed young. Soon it would be too late.

He continued to mutter while Sheilagh brooded resentfully.

Did he ever have a sister? And did she really die? When the clock struck seven she'd be off, and she shut both eyes, too drunk to know if she were dreaming or awake. He was still in his world of words, and they flew round her touching and stinging, just as always when she was as far gone as now. In a minute she was going to get up and walk out of his studio, art and life, and she wouldn't ever come back, not even if he begged, which he'd done before. His grief was inhuman, that's what it was, inhuman. Her upper lip twitched and she tried to get up. The trouble with Edwin was, drunk or sober, most of what he said sounded preposterous.

'I've been telling you for years I can't stand it...'

He didn't hear her because the voice was in his head again. 'Edwin.'

The voice was like waters breaking, the outburst of recumbent flats shivering their dykes in a frantic skirl. The place sloshed with the odour of bladder-vraic.

'Edwin.'

His sister scrutinised him like a fisherman breaking out a pearl. The waters gassed, pinking bubbles at the mouths of the bells, breasting the altar steps, bearing her up.

'Edwin, one day soon, I will claim you.'

How could Sheilagh know that Eddie's sister concluded her visitations to him every night with a vigil before the Madonna of the Indies, the thousands of bells about her swaying, and the sound of her bells was the sound of innumerable clashes of infinitesimal grains colliding in the shadow of the water-line?

Somewhere away, and inside what had been, and was still now, his sister lay in the manner of a postulant, her bells subsided, wreathed in her own bio-light, ungathered, raw as the earth. The place rocked around her, gently, in the lullaby motion of sea-swell, and the air keened through a gap in the great door flaring up the votive candles like wave-caps above the green casements of the sea, and everywhere the sea was penetrant, engulfing, scented with itself, which was the smell of her, and her nature.

He had to hold onto the canvas.

When he let go he fell over and left an entire palm-print impressed just below the sky-line of the picture.

Sheilagh ministered to him on the dais of the Life-room, covering him up to the throat with a heavy dustsheet and placing a cushion under his head. Not before, though, not before, and not for the first time, searching for and finding his wallet, from which she took exactly her due, no more, no less.

Rough

Gaia Holmes

You were never a Nivea guy,
but often sat with your elbows
soaking on cut potatoes
or with green avocado pulp
buttering your face.

Smooth, you were,
unlike me with my clumsy tongue,
my Brillo pad hands
and my fish-knife finger nails.

You read the wilderness in me.
Took note of the way
I could duck a wasp sting,
light fires with wet wood
and you tried to soften me,
imagined ironing out my voice,
dreamed me into chintzy parlors,
had me pouring tea
into fine bone china,
whispering to the aspidistra.

Rough, you used to say
when we were in bed
and my crusty heel
grazed your shin bone.
Too rough.
There was disapproval
in your tone.

Smooth

Gaia Holmes

He wants to show her off to his friends,
open her mouth and let them see
the solid curl of Kerrygold butter
that's not going to melt
on her chilled and temperate tongue.

He likes to believe
that the intellect she seems to lack
is fizzing somewhere deep in her subconscious
in a clever little room at the back of her brain
and it comes out in Latin
when she sleeps.

He imagines that her fantasies
are of chocolate box babies
and pruning and marriage
and brown paper parcels
but never of sex.

He wants parts of her
laser-printed onto his dinner plates,
wants to eat spaghetti bolognese off her face,
lick the gravy from the sills of her eyes,
suck the beef juice off her lips.

When he gets the chance
to get close enough
he will breath her in.
Her sweat will smell
of caramel and roses.

The Unknown Boxer Shorts

Katherine Spink

The waist band read 'Er Fun Boxer Fun B.'
The words were interrupted by seams at each side. The boxer's base colour was an uneven grey. She hoped that this tie dye effect was merely the result of frequent washing. There was a particularly dark patch over the groin area. She didn't inspect this too closely.

They were covered in pink lint spots. Tessie scrubbed at one with her nail. It didn't come off. She decided that the shorts must be polka dot. However, when she squinted at the spots in the light they looked like tiny pigs.

Disconcertingly, the boxers had a large image of a skeletal pelvis plastered over the front of them. When Tessie ran her hand over the image it was that horrible plasticky stuff that you get on cheap T-shirts. The stuff that your mum always manages to iron over and destroy. These shorts had so far escaped such a fate. The owner must do his own washing. Or have a mum who refuses to waste her time ironing her son's old boxer shorts. Tessie thought it was unusual to have pigs and a skeletal pelvis together on one pair of shorts. Surely that's too much novelty for any sane person?

Even more disconcerting was the presence of the boxer shorts in her bedroom. It was if they had appeared out of nowhere. Her feet had tangled in them in the middle of the night whilst she had been fetching a glass of water, the bony pelvis glaring at her in the dark like the search light of an alien space ship. Groggily, Tessie had booted them off her feet and climbed into bed. When she woke in the morning to the discordant tones of her alarm clock they had been on her pillow. An unpleasant 'Good morning,' finding someone else's underwear over your face.

Tessie took them into the kitchen with her to make some tea. They swamped on the counter like a disobedient pet. The angle of dangle showed the open fly, and she noticed they were missing a button.

Who would wear a pair of shorts like this?

Tessie hadn't tidied the bedroom in her flat for five months and in that time she had slept with three guys from college. These were the prime suspects.

She was surprised that she couldn't remember any of the boys she had been with wearing them. She was sure such bad taste would have stuck in her mind. She remembered reading somewhere that the sense of smell is the best sense for jogging the memory. She inhaled deeply, running her nostrils over the shorts. She could smell the faint Feta cheese tang of old sweat, mixed with cigarette smoke, and Chanel perfume. Not very helpful, seeing as the perfume and cigarettes were hers, and all men's pants smell like old cheese at the end of a long day.

Ok, so what do detectives do when they are looking for clues? On TV they always seem to touch things and lick their fingers. Taste must be the next big instrument in a detective's tool kit. Tessie bent over the shorts with her tongue out. She licked the waist band of the shorts, pulling the corners of her mouth down in a scowl of revulsion. She chewed her tongue. The shorts were bitty, 100% cotton. She could taste the powdery grit of washing powder. She spat and slurped four big gulps of watery tea to fight the dryness in her mouth.

So they can't be that dirty.

This was good. It meant that even when she couldn't remember the full details of a night out the men who came home with her were clean at the very least. Well, almost clean.

She decided to try the shorts on. Her English lecturer was always telling her to imagine things from someone else's perspective, walk a day in their shoes. Or in this case, walk five minutes in their pants. She pulled the shorts on up over the top of her jeans. She was only five foot and they billowed out almost to her knees. They must be extra large. They gaped open where the missing button was, exposing the stone washed denim beneath. She hopped about like she imagined a man running along the street in just his boxers might do. In her full length mirror she saw the pelvis jumping. It looked more like a cage of bone resting over her than the illusion of her own pelvis showing through. She took the boxers off and put them on her head, sweeping the short legs back in the style of a bandana, tucking her blond wavy hair into them.

While dancing about she glanced up at her mirror image again.

What am I doing?

She quickly pulled the pants off her head.

Who do I feel like in these?

The experiment hadn't worked. She felt like a prat. Every man she knew was a bit of a prat.

Her wrist watch beeped. Nine o'clock. Her first lecture started in thirty minutes.

She downed the rest of her tea and grabbed the boxers. Stuffing them in her bag she rattled out of the door.

* * *

On the way to college Tessie passed a thrift store. She stopped, her hand hovering over her bag where the unknown boxers were now nestled inside. The shop wasn't open yet and she would have to leave them on the step next to the sign that said 'Do not leave donations here.' She reached into her bag. The boxer shorts scurried away from her, hiding at the bottom. She groaned and started to empty some of the things out so she could reach them. She had to rest her weight on the skip outside the shop as she did so. A roll of discarded wall paper nudged her in the back from the safety of the skip. She managed to get the boxers out of the bag and they sat forlornly in her hands in the cold Autumn air, slumped in resignation. She peeped in to the skip to have a better look. James Bond books read a million times over and never to be read again, cracked and outdated earthenware pots, puzzles with all the corner pieces missing, holey clothes. Tessie couldn't bear to cast such a fate on her boxer shorts. If she could find their owner they may have a few years of good service left in them. She stuffed them back in to her bag and hurried on.

* * *

'You mean you don't know whose they are?' Connor and Tessie were standing outside the gym's changing rooms. He had the boxers in his hand and he looked upset.

Tessie chewed her lip and tried to make her eyes look bigger. Her usual injured puppy expression wasn't working on him today. The furrow between Connor's eyes depressed further into his forehead.

Connor must think I have had an army of boxer clad men in my room.

She pouted a little, and twisted her hair. Connor was shaking his head and his nose was wrinkled. The protective pads hugging his muscles made him look hard, not cuddly like she had so often thought.

I'm going to have to say something.

'No, no it's not like that. It's not like I've had tons of guys in my room or anything. I just don't remember whose they are.' After a pause she added, 'They could have been there for years.'

She put her hand over her mouth. That wasn't casting her in a very appealing light either.

Connor's team mates started filing out for rugby practice.

'They're not mine,' said Connor irritably, 'I'll put nametags on my clothes next time I come round.' He threw the boxer shorts back at her and they grabbed at her hair, caught there like a net.

That didn't go too well, thought Tessie as she peeled the shorts from her face. Although at least he didn't say he'd never come around again.

* * *

'Thank you Mrs Harrison,' Tessie accepted the glass of orange squash and held it between her knees as she sat on Jake's bed.

'If you two want anything else just let me know,' Jake's mum almost closed the door behind her, but left enough of a crack for someone to peep through, or for sounds to escape from the room easily.

'So...' said Jake.

'So...' said Tessie.

Asking outright obviously wasn't going to work. She had seen that with Connor. Now she had a theory. The theory was that anyone owning a pair of shorts this bad would have a whole array of novelty patterns and motifs hidden away in their underwear drawers. If there was a chance that a guy might get laid the likelihood is if he had only a few pairs of novelty underwear he would not wear a revolting pair out that night if he had any other options. However, if he only had horrible shorts he would have to wear them even on a night when he might be getting some. Logically then, if Jake was the culprit his drawers would be full of crap pants. And so, she was on a raid. Jake was also highest on the list of suspects because he was studying archaeology... or was it a palaeontology? She couldn't remember which, but it was some deadology anyway. Oh, and he was also in the chess club, and he still lived with his mum.

Time to divert him while she checked his underwear drawers.

'Do you think you could show me your fossil collection again? I found it really interesting last time,' she asked flicking her hair and smiling at him.

Jake beamed, 'Of course I can. Here...'

Jake passed her a selection of Chinese food boxes with rocks inside them. Not quite what she had in mind.

'Didn't you say that you had some big ones in the attic?'

'Yeah... just a few ammonites,' he slumped his shoulders. 'I can get them for you if you like.'

'Yeah, that would be great.'

Jake folded his long thin frame off the bed and sloped out of the door. She waited for a few seconds and then stealthily launched herself into his chest of drawers. First drawer... socks. Second draw... T-shirts. Bottom drawer... hosiery and knickers? Tessie blinked. She took a silky number out of the drawer and held it up to the light. The sun filtered through the lace, but beamed an 'O' through the crotch. Next she pulled out a violet pair of stockings, the belt still hanging from them. She delved through the drawer further, vainly looking for some manly underwear.

Jake walked back in.

'What are you doing?' He raced towards her, raising the

boulder sized ammonite as though he was going to hit her with it. She ducked away and ran out of the room.

'You dare tell anyone...' she heard him shout after her as she dodged passed his mum and pelted through the front door.

She walked home with her hand in the mouth of her bag fondling the skeleton motif thoughtfully.

They're not Jake's then.

* * *

Tessie sat in Solomon's kitchen with a mug of coffee. Solomon was older, thirty-one, and she thought he was a bit sad to be hanging out with college kids over ten years his junior. But being older, he might well be the owner of several awful pairs of boxer shorts, purely because he had experienced more Christmases in his lifetime than anyone else she had slept with. She listened to Solomon talk about himself for a while as she waited for her coffee to get cold enough not to scold him. Then she sloshed the coffee over his lap.

'What on earth did you do that for?' he asked her.

'It was an accident...'

'It didn't look like an accident. Kids!' he snorted, rubbing the knees of his coffee drenched slacks.

Tessie screwed up her eyes. She hadn't realised how obnoxious Solomon was before. She was surprised she had slept with him at all now she was actually having a conversation with him.

'Now I'm going to have to go and change my trousers,' he said, turning away.

'Wait! Why don't you take them off in here? You could just, you know... air them dry,' she said, giving what she hoped was a flirtatious smile. God, is he receding already? She wondered.

'They'll need washing. They reek of Gold Blend.' He looked up from his wet legs, caught Tessie's eye and smiled. 'I can't undress in front of you. You know what it'll lead to.' He winked at her.

'I just wanted to see what you were wearing underneath,' she said, while in her head trying to work out how she could escape once she had seen what sort of boxer shorts Solomon wore.

'Well,' he lowered his head and looked at her from under caterpillar eyebrows, 'If you really want to know... I'm wearing absolutely nothing underneath!'

He whipped off his trousers as though he were a magician revealing a neat trick. His penis was swaying at half mast like a worm popping out from the soil to see whether it was raining yet.

She screamed, grabbed her bag and legged it out the door again.

* * *

Tessie couldn't sleep. The shorts were on a coat hanger on the door knob of her cupboard. They were staring at her, the eerie glow-in-the-dark white of the bones moving and winking whenever she tossed her head to try and get comfortable. She had hoped that hanging them in view might help jog her memory, like when she was little and her parents had stuck posters of the eight and nine times tables on to every free wall space to make her remember them. Instead the boxer's mysterious nature had ended up invading her every thought, with no clue of their origin in sight.

Tessie sighed, gathered her duvet around her, and trudged into the lounge to sleep on the sofa away from them.

After the third night running of sleeping on the sofa Tessie decided there was only one thing to do. Even a remedial trip to the second hand shop wouldn't make her feel better. The shorts were plaguing her.

She took them to her shared back garden and set a circle of stones. She placed some dry grass in the circle and threw the shorts on top. She struck a match. A freak summer breeze sprang up and extinguished it. She tried again, and got as far as touching the grass with the flame before the match went out. Third time lucky and the kindling took. The flames licked at the shorts and at first Tessie thought they would be too stubborn for her little fire, but then they started to smoke under the heat. The cotton burnt away quickly, smelling like the ends of her scorched hair when she had once heat-sealed wool plaits into it. The motif spat and fizzed as though a demon lay within it, curling up like a fortune teller fish in your palm. She listened, and she could swear there was the faint sound of distressed oinks coming from the twisting fabric. They totally expired in a puff of purple smoke. Tessie sat huddled in front of the embers until they died away completely. Then she dispersed the stones and kicked the ashes across the grass.

She stood up and looked at the sky. She could make out the Plough and used it to guide her to the bright North Star. There were some threads of smoke still drifting in the air. Tessie smiled at the stars, at the planets, at the fact that now there was one less pair of novelty boxer shorts polluting underwear drawers across the world. With the death of the boxers she could turn over a new leaf, maybe even become a born again virgin. She had read about those on Wikipedia, along with baboons who could build radio transmitters.

* * *

The next morning her alarm blared and she struggled to wake. She swung her legs over the bed and put them down on the messy floor. Feeling dozy and drugged by sleep she slipped over in a tangle of clothes. Pulling the mishmash of clothing from her legs she came across an extra large T-shirt. She held it up in front of her letting the morning light stream from the window onto it. The T-shirt was one that she had never seen before, although there was something disturbingly familiar about it. It was black with small dots, and plastered across the front of it was a large motif of a glow-in-the-dark spine.

Rest

Lemn Sissay

'On the eve of the announcement of the Poet Laureate various poets were approached by Newsnight to give advice by verse. 'Rest' is mine. None of us officially knew who the laureate was at the time'

I expect you might at some point tonight
beneath the sheets before sleep
still reeling from the flaying lights,
want or more likely seek

rest. There is no manifesto in this
nor snake-like list of things to do.
There is no tomorrow either,
there's poetry as ever and you.

As Charles Bukowski Might Have Said

Jim Greenhalf

Human beings
                    like Tesco plastic carriers
are
                    100% degradable

                    like the sapphire miners of Madagascar
                    and others burrowing darkness
                    to scrape a living
disposable

but
                    unlike the levelled mountains of Kentucky
will endure.

Only mind the implications of that.

Contributors Biographical Notes

Penny Aldred won first prize in the Northern Echo/Orange short story competition in 2004. Her stories have appeared in *Aesthetica*, two Route anthologies, on BBC Radio 4's *Afternoon Reading* and turned into live art in Urbis as part of the Manchester Literature Festival 2007. She lives in West Yorkshire.

Timothy Allsop is an actor and writer. He was educated at Oxford University, Royal Holloway and the Guildhall School of Music and Drama. He has appeared on stage at the National Theatre, the Globe and Manchester Library Theatre amongst other venues. He has written for the stage and radio, and is currently completing a novel. He lives in London.

Simon Armitage was born in 1963 and lives in West Yorkshire. He has published nine volumes of poetry. His numerous awards include The Sunday Times Author of the Year, one of the first Forward Prizes and a Cannon Award.

Jonathan Asser is originator of Shame/Violence Intervention (SVI), a therapeutic programme that inhabits the dynamics of violent gang culture in prison. In 2008, SVI won the Innovation Award of the British Association for Counselling and Psychotherapy. Jonathan is also a poet (*Outside The All Stars, Arc, 2003*).

Nina Boyd is a student on the MA Poetry course at Manchester Metropolitan University. She has had a number of poems published, and is also working on a biography of a fellow-eccentric: Mary Sophia Allen, one of the first British policewomen.

John Boyne was born in Ireland in 1971. The winner of two Irish Book Awards, he has written seven novels including the international bestseller *The Boy In The Striped Pyjamas*, which was made into a Miramax feature film, and *The House of Special Purpose*, which is published in 2009. His novels are published in 40 languages.

Glenn Carmichael is from Darlington, County Durham. He now lives in Bristol. He has published a couple of poetry books, had a few short stories appear in magazines and had one novel published. He teaches performance poetry in schools and novel writing to adults. He likes to write and perform prose.

Glynis Charlton ditched the desk job to pursue freelance writing and these days moves from workshops to websites. Her work, known for its often bleak quality, has appeared in print, performance and on screen. She was shortlisted for the Bridport Poetry Prize in 2008 and is currently working on her second novel.

Ben Cheetham has had his fiction published in *The London Magazine, Staple, Dream Catcher, Transmission, Momaya Annual Review 2008, Swill* and numerous other magazines. He was runner up in this year's Willesden Herald International Short Story Prize. He recently completed his first novel for which he's seeking representation.

Brindley Hallam Dennis has won competitions at Radio Cumbria and *Cumbria Life* magazine, and Bank Street Writers & Grist prizes (2009). His work is published, broadcast and performed. An award winning poet writing as Mike Smith, he teaches Creative Writing at Cumbria University and has an MLitt from Glasgow University.

Kate Dempsey is from Coventry but now lives in Maynooth. Her poetry and fiction is widely published and she has been nominated for and won many prizes including The Francis MacManus and Hennessy New Irish Writing awards. She runs the Poetry Divas collective who are available to read at all cool festivals.

Paul Duncan is a sweet smelling, effervescent writer who was born in 1976. He resides in Leeds, and after a vigorous bout of education has recently graduated from university. In the future, he hopes to inflict his imagination on as many of the general population as is possible.

Fiona Durance has worked in dance, music, equalities training and as a BSL interpreter. She considers poetry the music of meaning, and particularly enjoys creative experimentation. Her work has appeared in many magazines and anthologies, and in theatres, galleries and on radio. Her writing has been placed in international competitions.

Gareth Durasow is a prize-winning poet and performer who runs with the mainstream hares and the avant-garde hounds. His work has appeared in numerous magazines and web-journals. In his spare time he helps run Letterbomb, a popular poetry open-mic night in Leeds, and he also writes for Horizon Arts theatre company; a job which pays enough to keep him in teaching.

Mark Ellis is a liar.

Len Evans began writing poetry as part of his counselling training in 1998. He's had poems published by CK Publishing and read publicly in Manchester, including a fundraiser for Christie's Hospital in 2008. He's inspired by Hughes, Donne and

R S Thomas and is hoping to start a new writers poetry group in Manchester.

David Gill is an award-winning songwriter and playwright, and the author of three books of poetry and three of fiction. He is currently specialising in the language and literature of song lyrics.

John Glander is one of those people to whom writing is rather like breathing and eating, a necessity. He has written and produced plays with school drama groups, published poetry and recently been placed in literary competitions. Though resident in Essex, his soul remains deeply rooted in his native Somerset.

Jim Greenhalf is a lyre – strung with piano wire.

Mick Haining came from the hills of Donegal to the flatness of Selby, used to teach Drama in the latter and now spends far too much time sedated by films. Nicola and the grown children are the jewels in his life.

Joanne Harris was born in Barnsley in 1964. She is the author of many novels including: *The Evil Seed, Chocolat, Blackberry Wine, Five Quarters of the Orange* and *The Lollipop Shoes*. Joanne has judged both The Whitbread and Orange Literary Prizes.

Beda Higgins publishes prose and poetry and is a future Booker Prize winner. In her spare time she works as a Practice Nurse and makes toast for her three children. She has five sisters, a twin brother and a St Bernard.

Gaia Holmes is Comma Press's most popular and successful poet. Her debut collection *Dr James Graham's Celestial Bed* was published to great acclaim in 2006. Eight poems from the book were adapted into films, one of which *'Desires'*, directed by Kate Jessop, was shortlisted for the Virgin Media Short Film Award.

Cath Humphris is a writer and part-time tutor in adult education. She has written plays for the amateur stage, adapted a novel for performance by university drama students and edited four non-fiction books. Right now, she is working on a series of short stories for younger readers.

Ruth Inglis is a final year student at the University of Huddersfield studying English Literature and Creative Writing. Her poem *Dreaming of Carpet Cleaner* is her first published work and she hopes it will not be her last. After graduating she intends to pursue a career in publishing while continuing to write in her spare time.

Skye Loneragan is an Australian writer/performer whose work includes the solo shows: *My Right Thumb, Cracked* (Edinburgh Fringe First), *Unsex Me Here* and *The Line We Draw*. She has performed a lot of her poetry and is currently working on a cross-artform residency with The Tramway, Glasgow.

Natalya Lowndes is the pseudonym of the art historian Sarah Symmons who teaches at the University of Essex. She published her first novel, *Chekago* (Hodder and Stoughton, 1988) to great critical acclaim. Since then she has published two further novels, short fiction and six non-fiction books.

Louis Malloy works as a computer programmer but prefers to write fiction. His short stories have been published in a variety of worthy magazines and he has won sufficient prize money to command an average annual writing income of £136.35. Like everyone, he is now writing a novel.

Andrew McMillan has been poet-in-residence of his own life since October 1988. His poetry has appeared widely in print and online magazines. He is co-editor of *Cake Literary Magazine* and his debut pamphlet is due in October 2009 from Red Squirrel Press.

Ian McMillan was born in 1956 near Barnsley. He has written many books of poetry as well as plays for radio and stage. He is the poet in residence at Barnsley Football Club. He also appears on Newsnight Review and presents *The Verb* on Radio 3.

Julie Mellor graduated from the University of Huddersfield in 1996. She went on to Sheffield Hallam where she gained an MA in Writing, followed by a PhD in 2003. Her work has appeared in *Brittle Star*, *London Magazine*, *Mslexia*, and *The Nerve* (Virago). She currently teaches English at a secondary school in Barnsley.

Hilary J Murray is a founder member of Borderstones Poets, Leeds; co-founder of Yorkshire women's poetry network EPIC. Poems feature in *Second Bite* (Grey Hen Press 2007), along with Joy Howard's and Gina Shaw's. The three of them perform as 'Second Bite' e.g. headlining the Poetry Alive! event at the 2009 Ilkley Literature Festival.

Karl O'Neill was born in Armagh, Northern Ireland, and is a professional actor based in Dublin. He has had short stories published in several periodicals and his children's book *The Most Beautiful Letter In The World* is published by O'Brien Press. He has recently completed his first novel, *August Time*.

Holly Oreschnick is currently studying Creative Writing at the University of Huddersfield. She has a deep interest in literature and poetry and has performed her poetry at many acclaimed venues around West Yorkshire. She has been a festival organiser for the Janet Beaumont Music and Drama festival and has taught English at Mara Primary School in Tanzania. She is very excited about being a part of the Grist Anthology.

Christopher Parvin lives in his head and holds a degree in Imaginative Writing from John Moores University. He has come third in the Ted Walters International Short Story Competition and is currently eating many a tonnage of finger nails writing his first novel. This will be his first published story.

Kyrill Potapov has written for print, stage and radio – each form retaining his unique and often quirky voice. The surreal acrobatics of his narrative call for an agile reader. The only thing one can predict about his stories, is that they will somehow involve cats and offer a musical experience.

Jess Richards is a writer who draws on mythology, fairy stories, psychology and the unconscious. She has written stories since childhood, but only recently and started to send them off. Since then three of her short stories have since been accepted for publication this year. She is now working on her first novel.

Lynn Roberts is an artist and art historian, and has co-written those riveting best-sellers, *A History of European Picture Frames and Frameworks* (1996). She has had poems published in *Outposts*, *Agenda*, *Envoi* and *LightenUp Online* and has just won the 2009 Listowel Writers' Week Poetry Collection competition.

Ami Roseingrave was born in Ireland and now lives in London with her husband and two children. Having taken time out from a career in research, she started writing fiction and began writing poetry eighteen months ago. Her work has been published by Ragged Raven, Ver Poets and Norwich Writers' Circle.

Jacquie Shanahan is an architectural publisher, with a Diploma in Creative Writing from Oxford University's Continuing Education Department. She's participated in poetry readings at Blackwells, and was shortlisted in a Radio Oxford short story competition. Jacquie is now completing her first novel, while studying for an MA at Manchester Metropolitan University.

Helen Simpson's first collection of short stories *Four Bare Legs in a Bed and Other Stories* (1990), won the Sunday Times Young Writer of the Year Award. There followed *Dear George, Hey Yeah Right Get a Life* (winner of the Hawthornden Prize and E.M.Forster Award) and *Constitutional*. Her fifth collection of stories will be published in 2010.

Lemn Sissay is the author of five poetry collections, his latest being *Listener*. He has also written for the stage and presented a six-part jazz series for the BBC. A documentary about Lemn's life called *Internal Flight* was recently broadcast on BBC One. He is a patron of the Huddersfield Literature Festival.

Katherine Spink lives in her own fantasy world where surreal things happen and odd behaviour is the norm. Occasionally she writes it down for other people to read. However, her story *The Unknown Boxer Shorts* is entirely fictional. Honest.

Kelly Stanger graduated from the University of Huddersfield with a first class honours degree in English with Creative Writing. In 2005 her poem *Market Kids* was shortlisted for the

Poetry Business competition and published in the Huddersfield Examiner. Kelly has performed her poetry at the Albert Hotel and the Beehive Inn.

Michael Stewart is a liar, a lyre and a lier, whose thoughts are strung on binding wire.

Andrea Tang graduated in 2008 with a first class honours degree from the University of Huddersfield in BA English Literature with Creative Writing. In 2008 she had micro-fiction and poetry published in competition anthologies by Leaf Books and Earlyworks Press. She was born in Malaysia, but resides in Huddersfield.

Anna-Marie Vickerstaff is inspired by Samuel Beckett, Gabriel Garcia Marquez, Jon McGregor, Franz Kafka and Stephen Chbosky. She is currently entering her final year on a BA in English Literature and Creative Writing course at the Univeristy of Huddersfield. In the future she hopes to write a dystopian novel, re-visit South Africa and grow rhubarb in her shed.

Martin Wickham has trained with Sir Alan Ayckbourn at the Stephen Joseph Theatre in Scarborough, studying script writing and acting. He was a member of the National Student Drama Festival ensemble in 2005 and won the Leeds Bright Young Things Music Competition in 2007. He is currently studying Creative Writing at the University of Huddersfield.